COIN DIVINATION

Pocket Fortuneteller

D1530053

With the Toss of a Coin . . .

. . . you can receive yes or no answers to questions, find out which choice is best from among several options, and even discover when future events will come to pass!

This little pocketbook is filled with divinatory techniques using coins—it includes many variations of the coin toss, and it also combines the coins with numerology, talking boards, tarot, dominoes, or the I Ching.

Divination with coins is simple, inexpensive, and portable. You can do readings for yourself and others anytime, anywhere. Put a fun new spin on fortunetelling with *Coin Divination*!

About the Author

Raymond Buckland is a Romany Gypsy and a leading authority on the Old Knowledge. He came to the United States from England in 1962 and has been actively involved in the study of the occult for over thirty-five years. In the past thirty years, he has had nearly thirty books published and has written numerous newspaper and magazine articles. He is the author of many best-selling books, including *Practical Candleburning Rituals* and *Practical Color Magick.*

To Write to the Author

If you wish to contact the author or would like more information about this book, please write to:

Raymond Buckland
% Llewellyn Worldwide
P.O. Box 64383, Dept. K089-2
St. Paul, MN 55164-0383, U.S.A.

Please enclose self-addressed stamped envelope for reply, or $1.00 to cover costs. If outside U.S.A., enclose international postal reply coupon.

COIN DIVINATION

Pocket Fortuneteller

Raymond Buckland

2000
Llewellyn Publications
St. Paul, Minnesota 5564-0383
U.S.A.

First Edition
First Printing, 2000

Book design and editing by Karin Simoneau
Cover design by William Merlin Cannon

Library of Congress Cataloging-in-Publication Data
Buckland, Raymond.
   Coin divination / Raymond Buckland
    p. cm.
   Includes bibliographical references (p.).
   ISBN 1-56718-089-2
    1. Divination. 2. Coins–Miscellanae. I. Title.

BF1779.C56 B83 2000
133.3–dc21   99-088433

Llewellyn Worldwide does not participate in, endorse, or have any authority or responsibility concerning private business transactions between our authors and the public.
   All mail addressed to the author is forwarded but the publisher cannot, unless specifically instructed by the author, give out an address or phone number.

Llewellyn Publications
A Division of Llewellyn Worldwide, Ltd.
P.O. Box 64383, Dept. K089-2
St. Paul, MN 55164-0383, U.S.A.
www.llewellyn.com

Printed in the United States of America

For my wife, Tara

Other Divination Books by Raymond Buckland

Secrets of Gypsy Fortunetelling (Llewellyn, 1988)

Gypsy Dream Dictionary (Llewellyn, 1998)

Secrets of Gypsy Love Magick (Llewellyn, 1990)

Gypsy Fortune Telling Tarot Kit (Llewellyn, book and deck, 1998)

The Buckland Gypsies' Domino Divination Deck (Llewellyn, 1995)

The Book of African Divination (with Kathleen Binger, Inner Traditions, 1992)

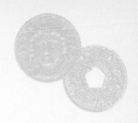

Contents

Introduction

In the seventh century B.C.E., the first coins were made—more than likely by the Lydians of Anatolia (Asia Minor). Their coins were made from a mixture of gold and silver—an alloy known as electrum—fashioned into a small disk. This disk was then imprinted by hitting a die placed on it. The first mint was established by King Croesus of Lydia. The Greeks, in the Aegean Islands, quickly picked up on this art of coinage and soon Italy, Persia, India, and other areas followed suit. At about the same time, coin making was taking place quite independently in the Far East—China, Japan, and Korea.

The first person to "flip" a coin "heads or tails?" is not known. Using just one coin, an unknown person discovered a wonderful way to arrive at a decision when faced with a choice between two things. This is almost certainly the simplest form of divination! It can be used in various ways and, with a number of coins, it's also possible to make a number of determinations and to become as proficient at the art of divining as is a tarot card reader or an astrologer.

Just what is "divination" and how does it work? Divination is so called because it is believed to be a gift from the divine—from the gods. There is evidence of its use by the Etruscans as far back as the first millennium B.C.E., though it was probably in use long before that. In earliest times it was frequently a matter of needing to know about the future of the hunting, or the crops, for the sake of survival. The sky was examined for signs of what might be coming, as were things like the movement of animals, the flight of birds, and even the direction of the wind.

Over thousands of years, these various forms of augury were refined and became the specialty of certain people—seers, augurers, prophets, and oracles. A wide variety of tools were used by these people as focal points and microcosms for determining the forces at work and how events might be affected. Today's tarot card reader, palm reader, or similar fortuneteller or diviner, is a descendant of those early seekers of knowledge. How accurate is divination? That is the major question, of course. Obviously, much depends upon the ability of the individual diviner. But this is an art that has survived for thousands of years; one that has persisted despite skepticism, attempted debunking, and religious persecution. Regarding the latter, divination is actually approved of and encouraged in the Bible, see 1 Corinthians 12: 4–12; 14: 1, 3, 31–32, 39; and Job 12: 7–8, for example.

Humankind has a fascination with the future and, in some cases, a *need* to know what the future holds; there seems to be as much of a demand for divination today as there ever was, despite our modern sophistication. This alone would seem an indication that there must be some truth to it. Certainly there are records of its accuracy too numerous to mention, with more coming literally every day. In this book, we look at the role that coins can play as tools of the diviner's trade.

While traveling around Britain, doing research for my various Gypsy books—*Gypsy Fortune Telling Tarot Kit; Secrets of Gypsy Love Magic; Gypsy Dream Dictionary; Gypsy Witchcraft and Magic*—I came across a number of people in different areas, and all used coins to practice one type of divination or another. Although not exclusively Gypsy in origin, many of the forms I present in this book I found primarily among the traveling people.

The Gypsies have developed a reputation as fortunetellers. They use cards (both tarot and regular playing cards), crystal balls, dominoes, dice, stones, and many other items; but the easiest objects to use are coins—for someone always has a few coins in their pocket. The Gypsies themselves carry their money with them (rather than entrust it to banks) and frequently wear gold coins as decoration on their clothing. It is quite probable that on certain occasions a Gypsy would divine using one or more of these gold coins—sovereigns and half-sovereigns, in Britain.

For anyone, using coins is a form of fortunetelling that is inexpensive, easily transportable, fascinating, and informative.

When considering the fascination of the subject, apart from the reading and divining, the very coins themselves can be appealing. I like to use foreign coins myself, especially those that are little known and perhaps even scarce. From the predecimal system British coinage, for example, the old farthings, half-pennies, pennies, and three-penny pieces are useful. You can go further and use coins that depict animals, for example, rather than those simply bearing people's heads, and the like. Many coins—particularly those from Asian countries, it seems—

depict birds, animals, and even insects. All of these can be worked into coin divination to produce the most interesting results. When choosing coins, don't overlook medals. There are many old medals that can serve beautifully as coins for divining. Good sources, for both medals and coins, are numismatic stores or coin shops, coin shows, pawnshops, and even yard sales.

Another possibility is religious medals. If you are attuned to Voodoun, Santeria, or Roman Catholicism, for example, then using medals depicting saints, angels, archangels, and the like, obtainable from religious supply stores and elsewhere, can be ideal. Sometimes these medals are available on a bracelet or necklace, from which they can be easily removed. Metaphysical mail order suppliers occasionally offer coins featuring talismanic designs.

The Chinese zodiac is depicted on the Republic of Singapore's ten singold coins—small, pure gold coins, each weighing one-tenth of an ounce. It is, therefore, possible to obtain a full set of twelve animal coins for little more than the cost of an ounce of gold (about $400.00 at the time of writing). For the serious practitioner, this provides beautiful divination tools and is also a wonderful investment.

Some gift catalogs—especially museum shop catalogs—offer reproductions of ancient coins: Roman, Greek, Hebrew, and so on. These can be very interesting replicas to use for coin divination.

The traveling people, and many of the others using coins, work at the very basic level. By that, I mean they take their coin(s) and divine when and as the need arises. However, as with tarot readers and others, some individuals like to make a complete ritual of a reading, feeling that in this way all possible forces are on their side. There is a lot to be said for this approach.

With coins, the start of the ritual is with the coin preparation. Any and all coins to be used should be ritually cleansed (see Part Five). They should then be wrapped in a piece of silk cloth or kept in a special pouch or bag made for the purpose. If you think it will be of benefit, incense may be burned during the reading to add to the positive vibrations.

Remove the coin(s) from the bag, hold them between the palms of your hands, and concentrate your thoughts on the question to be asked. (If you are religiously inclined, this is a good time to call upon your deity, or deities, to bless you with a clear decision.) If you intend to ask a number of questions, then this concentration should be done before each and every question. Clear your mind and aloud—in a firm, clear voice—ask the question and immediately throw, spin, or toss the coin(s).

But let's start at the beginning, with the single coin divination, and then go on to using two, three, or more coins.

Part One

COINS OF THE SAME DENOMINATION

YES OR NO ANSWERS TO QUESTIONS are the simplest and, oftentimes, the best answers. They are understandable and to the point, with no ambiguity. With a single coin, you can get your answer by tossing the coin or by spinning it.

Simple as it may seem, however, to be sure of getting the most accurate answer, make this uncomplicated act a ritual: take your coin from its bag and hold it between your cupped palms for a few moments while you concentrate on the question, then clear your mind and toss, or spin, the coin. Traditionally, heads is the equivalent of *yes* and tails of *no*.

But you can get more than a *yes/no* answer with just one coin.

3

One Coin

On a large sheet of paper, draw a circle about twelve inches in diameter. Draw a second concentric circle of about eighteen inches, and a third of about twenty-five inches:

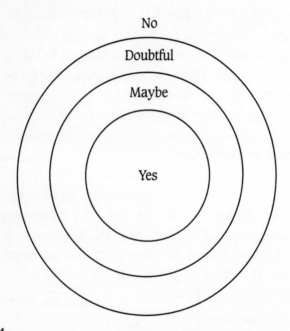

Throw your coin into the center of the circle. The innermost circle is a definite *yes* (regardless of whether the coin lands head-up or tail-up); the next largest circle is a strong *maybe*; the next circle is a *doubtful*; and outside the circle is a definite *no*.

You can adapt this circle system to ask about time; for example, "When will such-and-such happen?" Mark the center circle as being the Immediate Future (say, the next two or three weeks); the next circle would be Up To Three Months; the outer circle One Year, and outside the circles would mean Well Into The Future. You can mark the circles to suit the question you ask: you might want it to be in minutes and hours or in months and years.

In addition to these time scales, although the coin's landing heads or tails does not indicate *yes* or *no*, the face that is up may still be significant. A head-up landing would mean that the answer is directly applicable to the questioner (or the querant, if you ask on someone else's behalf), while a tail-up would mean that the answer will indirectly affect the questioner. A tail can also mean that although the answer is affirmative and shows the time period asked for, there will be an unexpected development, while a head means smooth sailing.

Another method is to draw one large circle (twelve to fifteen inches in diameter) and draw a center line, running away from you, bisecting it in half. Then, across that line and the circle, draw two other lines, equally spaced, as shown.

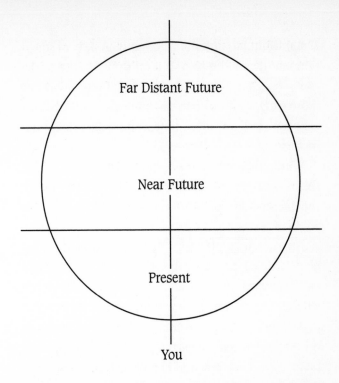

Far Distant Future

Near Future

Present

You

The vertical line running away from you represents you (or the querant). The two bisecting lines break down the divination area into the Present (closest to you), Near Future (the center section), and Far

Distant Future (furthest from you). Ask your question and throw the coin. If it falls outside the circle, throw it again. If it falls outside again, throw it one more time. You have three chances. If it falls outside the circle all three times, the question cannot be answered at this time.

Within the circle, the closer to the main line it falls, the more significant the answer and the more you (or the querant) are affected. The further out toward the edges of the circle, the less influence it has on you.

Another way of using a coin is to use it as the planchette of a talking board. Cut out thirty-eight small squares of paper and mark twenty-six with a letter of the alphabet, ten with the numbers from 1 to 0, and two with the words *yes* and *no*. Lay these thirty-eight pieces of paper in a circle on top of a table, so it looks like a talking board (or Ouija). The paper does not have to be right at the edge of the table, as long as it is in a circle. Now throw the coin. Whether it falls within the circle or outside of it, determine the letter or number closest to where it falls and then throw it again. In this way, as with the planchette of a talking board, you can spell out messages and obtain information. For more information on talking boards and their idiosyncrasies, see my book *Doors To Other Worlds* (Llewellyn, 1992).

One of the many joys of coin divination is that you can do it almost anywhere. You can even do it while walking. Ask your question as you walk, then simply reach into your pocket and pull out a coin. Again, heads is *yes* and tails is *no*.

You can also use one coin together with a deck of cards for foretelling the future. Take out the Ace of Clubs, King of Diamonds, Jack of Hearts, Jack of Spades, Five of Clubs, and Two of Diamonds and, after shuffling them, lay them face down on a table, as shown.

Take the coin in your hands and shake it up, then drop it (from a height of about twelve inches) onto the cards. Turn face-up the card on which it falls, or the one to which it is closest. If it falls equidistant from two or more cards, then drop it again. You have three chances. If it falls equidistant from more than one card every time, you cannot answer at this time. Below are the traditional meanings for the results:

	Head	Tail
Ace of Clubs	Beware of severe losses through recklessness.	A gift of considerable value will come from a stranger.
King of Diamonds	Avoid all financial transactions for the next two days.	An unexpected pay raise is coming.

	Head	**Tail**
Jack of Spades	Loss because of theft or carelessness on your part.	A quarrel over a small amount of money.
Jack of Hearts	Responsibility will be brought about by an unexpected sum of money.	Be on guard against some well-intended advice regarding your finances.
Five of Clubs	Someone will entrust you with valuable property.	Save now for hard times ahead.
Two of Diamonds	A talent you had forgotten is going to prove very profitable to you.	You are going to have some good luck in regard to money.

If you have a question with several possible answers and want to know which is the best, you can take index cards, or squares of paper, and write each possibility on a separate card. Then, as above, shuffle them and lay them out, face down. Concentrate on the question as you shake the coin. Let it fall—the card it lands on, or nearest to, is the answer to the question.

Two Coins

Two coins can give you four variables: head and tail; tail and head; head and head; and tail and tail. In order to differentiate between the tail and head and the head and tail, of course, you need to consistently *read* the coins from left to right, or vice versa—it doesn't matter which way you read them as long as you are consistent. With a *yes/no* question, using two coins, you can read two heads as *yes*, two tails as *no*, and either head and tail or tail and head as *maybe*. You can also say that head and tail is *maybe* and tail and head is either "Rephrase the Question" or "Cannot Answer." Again, such a reading can be done even when out walking.

Using the method of the circle with the central dividing line and three cross areas (see page 7), you can throw the two coins and get a lot of information. First of all, the heads indicate positive energies and the tails negative energies. The closer to the main central line either or both fall, the more those energies have an effect on the questioner. Again, as above, the nearest area represents the Present, the middle area is the Near Future, and the far area is the Far Distant Future. Let's take an example of one coin falling head-up close to the central line, in the nearest area, and the other coin falling tail-up, almost on the outer line of the circle, in the middle area.

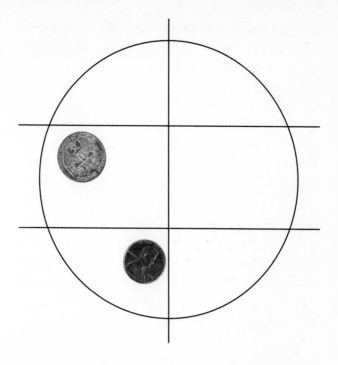

From what has been said about the meanings of the areas, this example indicates that there are very positive energies closely affecting the questioner at the present moment, but there are also some negative energies that, in the near future, will be coming in; however, the negative energies are not too close to the individual, so will only have a slight effect on the person.

Three Coins

In *Gypsy Witchcraft and Magic* (Llewellyn, 1998), I detailed a method of divining using three similar coins. In fact, it was this particular method that first started my interest in coin divination.

The *reader* holds the three coins and concentrates on the question. The coins are then thrown and their relative positions are noted. First of all, the head and tail revelation is interpreted. With three coins there are eight possible combinations:

1: Head, Tail, Tail

2: Head, Head, Tail

3: Head, Head, Head

4: Tail, Tail, Tail

5: Tail, Tail, Head

6: Tail, Head, Head

7: Head, Tail, Head

8: Tail, Head, Tail

Again, we are regarding the coins as being as close to a straight line as possible. The interpretations are as follows:

Head-Tail-Tail: Possibly negative. Possibility of trickery. Be on your guard. Plan carefully. Bad investments. Opportunities, if you choose carefully.

Head-Head-Tail: Possibly positive. Potential for gain. Chance to invest. Possibility of love.

Head-Head-Head: Definitely positive. Joy and contentment. Wishes fulfilled. Enjoy yourself. Fertility.

Tail-Tail-Tail: Definitely negative. Tragedy. Bad luck. Fraud. Scandal. Seduction.

Tail-Tail-Head: Possibly negative. Exercise caution. Possibility of bad news. Financial loss. Accusations.

Tail-Head-Head: Possibly positive. A letter containing good news. Meeting with an old friend. Business success. Inheritance.

Head-Tail-Head: Possibly positive. Meeting with a person that could be very fortunate. A new beginning; a chance to start over.

Tail-Head-Tail: Possibly negative. Meeting with a person who should not be trusted. Temptation. Plan before acting.

These are basic, quick readings. Depending upon the lie of the coins and their separation from each other, the readings can be elaborated. For example, the closer two tails are together, the more negative there is present; the closer two heads are together, the more positive there is present. When two tails are close together but lying some distance from the head, then there is more of a balance of positive and negative, despite the double tails. Similarly, two heads together some distance from a tail balances the forces.

If you look at the heads and tails from the yin/yang perspective, rather than the good/bad polarity, it can make the reading very interesting— yin/yang being the duality of the cosmos; together, they represent the dynamic duality and interaction that brings about reality.

Yin is yielding while yang is firm. Let's equate heads with yang and tails with yin.

Head-Tail-Tail: Flexibility. Detachment. Step back to see the whole picture. Ability to change, though persuasion may be necessary.

Head-Head-Tail: Obstacles, but not insurmountable. Firmness needed, but be ready to give a little if necessary.

Head-Head-Head: Super yang. Your influence is at a maximum. Outward flow of energy. Firmness and action are required. Lessons to be learned.

Tail-Tail-Tail: Super yin. A time to concentrate your energy. Less movement and more rest or contemplation is advised. Stillness. Your influence cannot be felt. Retreat. Beware of being too flexible. A time for creation and also completion.

Tail-Tail-Head: Limitations. Be aware of overexertion. Don't take on too much.

Tail-Head-Head: Be very aware of your inner feelings—your intuition. It won't lead you wrong. A good time for new beginnings.

Head-Tail-Head: Gather your forces. Draw on friends and family for needed extra strength. Alone you're vulnerable; with others you're invincible.

Tail-Head-Tail: Avoid confrontation. Keep in the background. Discretion is the better part of valor.

When the coins are grouped together in a perfect triangle, very close to each other, this indicates money. When they are in a wide, but equally spaced, triangle, then legal matters may be likely—possibly a lawsuit. When the coins are in a perfectly straight line, all equidistant apart, this indicates a journey. In an equally spaced curve, there can be delays.

Five Coins for Numerology

Numerology can be used for many things, including answering questions and getting impressions of people. The basis of all numbers and calculations are the numbers 1 through 9, since any number can be reduced to one of these primary numbers. With coin divination we work with five coins, giving each head the value of 1 and each tail the value of 2. If we throw down the five coins and get, say, three heads and two tails, that would be $1 + 1 + 1 + 2 + 2 = 7$. Similarly, one head and four tails would give $1 + 2 + 2 + 2 + 2 = 9$. If we got five tails ($2 + 2 + 2 + 2 + 2$), we would have 10 but, in coin divination, this is taken as 0, since we work only with 1, 2, 3, 4, 5, 6, 7, 8, 9.

For the divination process, draw a small circle, about six inches in diameter. Shake up the coins and drop them onto the circle. They may not all fall within it; some may roll out. Of those that *do* fall inside, add up the heads and tails. For example, suppose three coins fall inside the circle, two of them landing head side up and one tail side up. That is $1 + 1 + 2 = 4$. Another example: suppose four coins land inside, two heads and two tails. That would be $1 + 1 + 2 + 2 = 6$. These numbers can give you answers to questions you may ask.

Let's look, first of all, at the meanings of the resultant numbers.

1: A driving force; a leader. Ambitious and tending to be impatient to get things done. Automatically assumes command. The extrovert. Frequently a "big brother" or "big sister." Often has very strong feelings either for or against; seldom middle of the road. Would not knowingly hurt anyone but does not realize own strength. Praise can spur to greater efforts. Associated with the Sun.

2: Sensitive and domestic. Can become emotional. Has fertile imagination. Fond of the home and family. Easily accepts changes in surroundings. Fond of water and likes to live near it. Frequently musically inclined. Often psychic. Associated with the Moon.

3: The seeker; the investigator. Often involved in science. More material than spiritual, though not especially interested in money. Good sense of humor. Very trusting but likes to understand what makes things tick. Ideas on religion frequently changing. Associated with Jupiter.

4: Often ahead of their time. May appear strange or eccentric. Great interest in matters metaphysical. Strong intuitive tendencies; frequently psychic. Drawn to anything out of the ordinary. Can become sarcastic, if pressured. Believes in liberty and equality. Associated with Uranus.

5: Mentally and physically active. Asks lots of questions; always searching for answers. Good at languages and would make a good teacher or writer. Makes friends easily. Methodical and orderly; good at simplifying systems. Associated with Mercury.

6: Gentle, refined, pleasant and sociable. A natural peacemaker and diplomat. Not comfortable with finances. Often good-looking. A good host or hostess. Associated with Venus.

7: Extremely psychic. An introvert. Knows a great deal but does not speak a lot. Can be mysterious, with an interest in chemistry and psychology. Also knowledgeable in astrology and the occult. Likes to take from the "haves" to give to the "have-nots." Associated with Neptune.

8: Often pessimistic and seemingly cold, with little sense of humor. Though slow getting started, can often surprise by finishing ahead. Good with finances. Interested in mining, real estate, and the law. Believes in hard work. Fascinated by the past, and by cemeteries. Associated with Saturn.

9: Can be very emotional and often jealous. Active, though ruled by the emotions. Tied to family background. Can be extremely loyal. Suspicious of strangers. A fear of the unknown. Often associated with surgery and with physical and mental illnesses. Associated with Mars.

If you have questions about a person, the above will give you a good idea of what they are like, based on the coins that land in the circle when you ask about them.

You can also get answers to a variety of questions. Suppose you are thinking of relocating to, say, Florida. You can find the numerological value of Florida, using the letters of the alphabet aligned with the numbers 1 through 9, thus:

1	2	3	4	5	6	7	8	9
A	B	C	D	E	F	G	H	I
J	K	L	M	N	O	P	Q	R
S	T	U	V	W	X	Y	Z	

From this, Florida is F = 6, L = 3, O = 6, R = 9, I = 9, D = 4, A = 1. 6 + 3 + 6 + 9 + 9 + 4 + 1 = 38. This can be further reduced to one digit by adding: 3 + 8 = 11, then 1 + 1 = 2. So the numerological value of Florida is 2.

Now throw your coins into the circle, and concentrate on whether or not Florida would be a good place to relocate. If you get two heads (1 + 1) or just one tail (2), then you have confirmation that it would be a very good move. Obviously, for such a question, you need to take many other factors into consideration, but a "2" throw would certainly indicate that Florida would be an excellent choice.

For a basic *yes/no* question, if the coins give you an odd number, that is a *yes*; an even number is a *no*.

Want to know what color to paint your apartment? Throw the coins and see! The affinity of colors to numbers is as follows:

1: brown, yellow, gold

2: green, cream, white

3: mauve, violet, lilac

4: blue, gray

5: *light* shades of any color

6: all shades of blue

7: *light* shades of green and yellow

8: dark gray, blue, purple, black

9: pink, red, crimson

Numerology is a fascinating study and there are many good books written about it (see Bibliography). Experiment using coins to arrive at the necessary numbers.

Part Two

COINS OF DIFFERENT DENOMINATIONS

WITH UNITED STATES COINAGE, you could use a nickel, a dime, a quarter, and a Susan B. Anthony dollar as four different coins. A fifty-cent piece might also be used, but a large silver dollar might be considered too heavy. From British coinage, you could use the penny, twopence, five, ten, twenty, and fifty pence. The pound would be a little heavy, but could also be used. Of the old-style British coinage, you have a choice of the farthing, halfpenny, penny, threepenny piece, sixpence, shilling, florin, and half-crown. Other countries' denominations can be used just as well. Of course, there's no reason why you shouldn't mix and match, which might be a very good idea in that you could have a number of different coins but all of similar size and weight.

For the sake of examples in this chapter, I will simply term the different coins A, B, C, and so on. For example, A might be an older British florin, B might be a United States quarter, and C a French centime.

Two Coins

If you are trying to make a choice between two alternatives, let one coin (coin A) represent one of the choices and the other coin (coin B) represent the other choice. Throw the coins; the one that lands closer to you is usually the better choice. (This can also be done with three or more different coins, of course, representing more choices. In this way, you can grade from the best choice to the worst.)

The one that lands closer is *usually* the better choice. That's because you might throw them and, although A landed closer, it might be a tail, while B, landing farther away, would be a head. If you look at heads as being positive and tails as negative, then from that throw you would say that although A is the better choice initially, it could lead to a less desirable situation; and although B was indicated (by virtue of landing farther away from you) as being the worse choice, it could eventually turn out to be better! So, you see, you need to not only consider the positions of the coins, but also whether they land head-up or tail-up.

Three Coins

You can use three coins of different sizes. Let's say, for example, a nickel, a dime, and a quarter. Throw them down and look at the head and tail combinations, regardless of where they fall (in other words, they do not have to be in a straight line). The possibilities are as follows:

Nickel	Dime	Quarter	Reading
Head	Head	Head	Very positive. Plans will succeed. Good news coming.

Nickel	Dime	Quarter	Reading
Head	Head	Tail	Things look promising, but take care; watch where you tread.
Head	Tail	Tail	Things may look black, but there is a silver lining on the gray clouds. Hold on.
Tail	Tail	Tail	Negative energies around you.
Tail	Tail	Head	There will be a period of negativity, but it will eventually give way to positive energies.
Tail	Head	Head	Bad luck at the moment so invest for the future, not the present.

| Head | Tail | Head | | Everything may seem rosy, but look carefully for the hidden enemy. |
| Tail | Head | Tail | | Intrigue is all around you, but hold on to your ideals; you will be proven right. |

Four Coins

For general fortunetelling or divining, ask your question and shake the four coins. Drop them onto the table. The possibilities are increased to sixteen, as follows:

A	B	C	D	Reading
Head	Head	Head	Head	Wisdom.
Head	Head	Head	Tail	Here is power. Act now but don't be domineering.

35

A	B	C	D	Reading
Head	Head	Tail	Tail	Listen to advice of others; seek help.
Head	Tail	Tail	Tail	Possible ills; things are weak.
Tail	Tail	Tail	Tail	No. Could have a serious loss.
Head	Head	Tail	Head	Something not right. Illusions.
Head	Tail	Head	Head	Listen to self; rely on intuition.
Tail	Head	Head	Head	Feeling trapped; be watchful for deceit.
Head	Tail	Head	Tail	New things now: babies, jobs, and opportunities.

Tail	Tail	Head	Head	Escape. Correct problems.
Tail	Tail	Tail	Head	Incomplete; need to learn.
Head	Tail	Tail	Head	Need hard work—here is strength.
Tail	Head	Tail	Head	Time to travel and to expand; changes.
Tail	Head	Head	Tail	Hiding from reality; great calm.
Tail	Tail	Head	Tail	Spirituality high; naiveté.
Tail	Head	Tail	Tail	Time to think before action.

Astrological Coins

An interesting astrological reading can be obtained by taking ten coins to represent the planets and throwing them down on a chart of the Houses of the Zodiac:

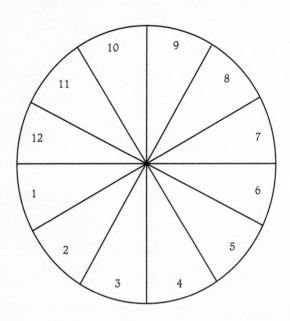

Let's call the coins A, B, C, D, E, F, G, H, I, and J, and let's equate them to the planets:

A = SUN: A masculine planet, full of vitality. Determination yet much kindness; a lot of heart; capable of great love. An authoritative figure, ever moving forward.

B = MOON: A feminine figure. Very sensitive and emotional. Domestic. A lover of water. Patriotic and interested in public welfare.

C = MERCURY: Quick-witted. An extremely active mind. Good at research, exploration, analysis, and judgment. Associated with writers, teachers, and orators.

D = VENUS: Feminine; very much of love. Associated with friendship, physical attraction, peacemaking, feeling, and pleasure. Associated with musicians, jewelers, actors, artists, and nurses.

E = MARS: Action, energy, and courage. Can be brutal and jealous. Sometimes the cause of sexual problems. Impulsive, loyal, and afraid of the unknown. Associated with the military, surgeons, sportsmen, and craftsmen.

F = JUPITER: Harmony, law, education, morals, and religious faith. Truth comes first. Good humor, knowledge, and the ability to self-educate; learning through reading. Associated with bankers, judges, and ecclesiastics.

G = SATURN: Inhibited, persevering, and cautious. Often frustrated, reserved, and taciturn. Associated with the law, mining, printing, dentistry, building, real estate, secondhand goods, agriculture, and death.

H = URANUS: Excitable and erratic. Inclined to be sarcastic. Often too forceful. An affinity with nature and also with technical objects. Associated with electricians, inventors, and astrologers. Very much of the occult.

I = NEPTUNE: Inclined to mysticism and individuality. Knows but does not speak. Can be capable of rape, and even murder. Sometimes vague or confused. Associated with restaurants, bars, prostitution, narcotics, navigation, the ocean, nursing, and advertising.

J = PLUTO: Associated with youth and young children. People wanting things their own way. Leaders. A dislike of laws. Associated with sports, hobbies, outdoor life, actors, and politicians.

It may help to engrave each coin with its planetary symbol (see Part Five), otherwise, it will probably call for the use of pencil and paper to keep account of what goes where and what the meanings are! Assign a coin to each planet, shake them, and throw them down on the drawn layout of the Zodiacal Wheel of the Houses.

House 1 is associated with your self-image and the role that you adopt in life in your formative years. Part of the body associated: the head.

House 2 is the house of material possessions. Body part: the neck.

House 3 deals with sibling relationships, communications, and short journeys. Body parts: the shoulders, arms, and lungs.

House 4 is of the home, childhood, and your roots. It also deals with your mother and old age. Body part: the chest.

House 5 is the house of creativity and of children, love, and entertainment. Body parts: the heart and circulatory system.

House 6 deals with your capacity to work and with your health. Body part: the upper abdomen.

House 7 is that of partnerships, business, and love and marriage. Body parts: the lower abdomen and digestive system.

House 8 is birth, death, regeneration, and other people's resources. Transformation and the occult are also found here. Body part: the generative organs.

House 9 is the house of education, religion, philosophy, and travel, including long journeys. Body part: the thighs.

House 10 is of career and social achievement. It also deals with the underworld. Body part: the knees.

House 11 is groups and societies; ideals and aspirations. Your hopes, your wishes, and your friends. Body parts: calves and ankles.

House 12 is the house of things "locked away"— your unconscious mind. It also deals with karma, secret enemies, and hospitals. Body part: the feet.

By throwing the coins, you will obtain positions of the planets in the houses. Not all the coins will necessarily fall into the wheel (make the wheel a good size, so you can get a number of coins within it). Ignore those that fall outside—only read those that land inside. When the coin lands head-up, it is a "well aspected" sign; if tail-up, then it is called, in astrological terms, "under affliction." A good book on astrology will give you the full meanings of the planets through the twelve houses, but here are the basic meanings.

Sun in First House: An inward-looking tendency. Possible selfishness. Well aspected (heads) shows good health; afflicted (tails) shows there is the chance of bad health.

Sun in Second House: Focus is on finances, with an urge to earn more money. A desire to gather material wealth, so beware of becoming possessive. Force yourself to share with others.

Sun in Third House: A fascinating speaker and competent writer. Communication is important. An interest in education. Try not to be impatient; develop persistence.

44

Sun in Fourth House: Well aspected shows great happiness with home life, while afflicted shows discontent. Tendency to be introspective. Strong family ties. Seeking security.

Sun in Fifth House: Very positive. Great enjoyment derived from the home and family and from life in general. A fondness for children. Seeking romance and power. Be careful not to take risks, especially with family finances.

Sun in Sixth House: Well aspected indicates excellent health. Very good organizational ability; chance of advancement in business. Afflicted would indicate unsuitability to lead and direct others. Can be too demanding of coworkers.

Sun in Seventh House: Excellent for partnerships, whether business or personal, though a tendency to dominate the partnership. Regard social status as important.

Sun in Eighth House: Deep interest in metaphysics, the occult, and New Age. Possible involvement with the financial affairs of other people. Possibility of an inheritance.

Sun in Ninth House: A desire to study, which should be followed. Foreign languages could come easily. Possibility of travel abroad. A need for security.

Sun in Tenth House: Absorption in career, bringing enjoyment and satisfaction. A desire to succeed; can be power-driven. Beware of neglecting other aspects important to your life (a strong tendency to do so if afflicted).

Sun in Eleventh House: Opportunity to be elected to office of some sort. Well aspected especially good for this. Good chance to demonstrate organizational abilities. Growth of a friendship and learning experience, but beware of becoming argumentative.

Sun in Twelfth House: Introspective, particularly where business is concerned. Secretive work. Medical work worthwhile. A time not to share all thoughts with partners.

Moon in First House: Maternal nature is strong. Imagination is good. There is a shrewdness in business matters. Can be tenacious at this time. Beware of becoming narrow-minded. Can be changeable and moody.

Moon in Second House: Instinct to save money. Fluctuations in income at this time. Must learn to budget.

Moon in Third House: Changes in educational experiences. Need to communicate. Protective attitude to younger siblings. Travel-minded.

Moon in Fourth House: Afflicted shows a clinging attitude toward children. Inclined to worship ancestors; an interest in history. An urge to redecorate or even relocate.

Moon in Fifth House: Sport activity, possibly leading to fame. Interest in gambling; to be avoided if afflicted. Love of children and large families. Love affairs.

Moon in Sixth House: Hygiene and cleanliness—especially in the home—is very important. Reduced vitality. Try not to be too critical of others' work patterns.

Moon in Seventh House: Desire for social success. Very status conscious. Need for a partner, though attracted to moody partners. Emphasis on relationships with women. Afflicted indicates unsteadiness in business. Well aspected indicates firmness of business status.

Moon in Eighth House: Preoccupation with sex. Interest in the afterlife. Possible involvement in public finance. Psychic powers.

Moon in Ninth House: Travel-minded. Attracted to ancient history and, in particular, dead languages. Foreign travel, or even relocation, possible. Consider changes in religious ideas.

Moon in Tenth House: Changes in occupation considered. Concerned with reputation; seeking public recognition. Brief fame likely. Afflicted indicates loss of privacy.

Moon in Eleventh House: Large number of friends and acquaintances. Varied interests. Well aspected indicates a deep interest and involvement in a variety of societies and associations. Afflicted indicates many passing interests and superficial involvement.

Moon in Twelfth House: Respite or sabbatical sought. Need for retirement, if only temporarily. Retreating into the imagination: detrimental under affliction but beneficial when well aspected. Strong psychic and mediumistic abilities.

Mercury in First House: Emphasis on intellectual energy. High-strung with quick reactions. If afflicted, beware of becoming too self-centered. Excellent communication skills.

Mercury in Second House: Strong business aptitude. Financial skills. Excellent bargaining powers. Potential to become very good salesperson.

Mercury in Third House: Active and restless. Change in love. Looking for travel opportunities. Intellectual. Talkative. If under affliction, nervous system could be of concern.

Mercury in Fourth House: Home study and work. Tendency to hold on to old, and often useless, items from the past. Can become overly domesticated.

Mercury in Fifth House: Good at games involving mental activity and strategy. Creative. Teaching ability. Good rapport with young people and children.

Mercury in Sixth House: Beware of mental anxiety. Overconcern with health matters. Possibility of intestinal problems. If afflicted, self-destructive tendencies.

Mercury in Seventh House: Attracted to those younger than yourself. Need intellectual stimulation, especially in partners. Scientific, literary, and artistic interests.

Mercury in Eighth House: Interest in the occult. If afflicted, preoccupation with death. Scientific leanings. Carefully read the fine print before signing any documents.

Mercury in Ninth House: Intuitive. Broad-minded and interested in traveling. A need for self-expression. Languages attract, as does higher education.

Mercury in Tenth House: A career in publishing, or anything connected with the literary world, would be beneficial. Good communications. Keep busy or grow restless.

Mercury in Eleventh House: Under affliction, beware of unreliable friends. Need mental stimulation. Look for a lively social life.

Mercury in Twelfth House: Tendency to fantasize—try to fix more on reality. Worry too much. Try not to be too secretive. An attraction to mysticism.

Venus in First House: Charming, good-looking, and sexy. If afflicted, can become too self-centered, lazy, and spoiled. Fond of music and drama.

Venus in Second House: Obsessed with acquisitions. Extravagant. Sociable and pleasure-loving. Capable of building up finances.

Venus in Third House: Good relationships with siblings. Excellent at expressing ideas. Happy disposition. Ability to study.

Venus in Fourth House: Good at interior decorating. Able to express ideas. Love to travel. Beware of extravagance.

Venus in Fifth House: Enjoy sports, games, creativity, and the arts. Inclined to have sexual love affairs. Musical ability. Enjoy children.

Venus in Sixth House: Enjoy good health. Get along well with coworkers. Fond of animals. In very good health.

Venus in Seventh House: If well aspected, excellent for starting partnership relationship (business or personal). If afflicted, persecution complex may materialize.

Venus in Eighth House: Inheritance possible. Strong sex drive—satisfied if well aspected but frustrated if afflicted.

Venus in Ninth House: Lover of travel and good relationships with foreigners. Idealistic and sympathetic. May develop interests in religion. Good, smooth marriage.

Venus in Tenth House: Popular. Successful in business; ambitions realized. If well aspected, good relationship with parents, but problems if afflicted.

Venus in Eleventh House: Friendships could lead to profits and advantages. Good time to work with groups and organizations. Many friends.

Venus in Twelfth House: A need to be alone for a while. Love of animals. Possible secret love affair. Interest in the occult.

Mars in First House: Freedom-loving. A pioneer. Give positive and immediate response to situations that arise. If afflicted, can be quarrelsome, aggressive, and lack forethought.

Mars in Second House: Can make money quickly, but can lose it just as quickly. Learn to budget and plan. Don't try to appear the big spender.

Mars in Third House: Beware of taking too many risks. Not always logical; can be too hasty. If afflicted, watch tendency to become too aggressive.

Mars in Fourth House: If well aspected, hard-working and handy at home. Under affliction there is a yearning to get away and to be independent. Possible losses in real estate.

Mars in Fifth House: Get along well with children. Beware of desires to constantly gamble. Beware of tendency for self-indulgence.

Mars in Sixth House: Watch your health; subject to fevers, inflammations, cuts, and small wounds at this time. Good, industrious worker. Don't push coworkers too hard.

Mars in Seventh House: Well aspected indicates energy and good cooperation with partners. Under affliction indicates quarrels and disappointments. May lose partner.

Mars in Eighth House: Involvement with insurance. An interest in surgery. If well aspected, strongly sexed at this time. If afflicted, there could be difficulties with legal matters.

Mars in Ninth House: A love of travel, but beware of possible danger in foreign travel. Good time to indulge in sports. Mentally alert.

Mars in Tenth House: Very energetic. Very ambitious, with a great desire to be your own boss. If afflicted, trouble with parents.

Mars in Eleventh House: Much activity with friends, but this is a time when you may lose some of them, so try to control impulsive behavior. Much energy and enthusiasm.

Mars in Twelfth House: Very secretive. If well aspected, a great desire to help others. If afflicted, a possible loss of reputation. Watch out for treachery.

Jupiter in First House: Able to inspire others and have great vitality. If well aspected, you can be optimistic, generous, and loyal. If afflicted—wasteful, conceited, and self-indulgent.

Jupiter in Second House: Financially successful, though inclined to extravagance. If under affliction, beware of financial carelessness.

Jupiter in Third House: Good relationship with family, especially siblings. Enjoyment of the learning process. Interested in literature and travel. Communication is good.

Jupiter in Fourth House: Love of pomp and ceremony. Very good home conditions. Possible vanity and lack of perspective.

Jupiter in Fifth House: Pleasure-loving. Enjoy art, literature, and theater. Some ability in sport. If well aspected, could take financial chances and come out ahead. If afflicted, stay away from gambling!

Jupiter in Sixth House: Good health, but if afflicted, may be inclined to hypochondria. Observe good eating habits. Loyal and cooperative. If well aspected, plenty of work increases finances.

Jupiter in Seventh House: Very good for business partnerships. Not necessarily a happy home life. If afflicted, strict control needed when attracted to sex outside marriage.

Jupiter in Eighth House: Inheritance possible, either money or property. Interest in life after death. Ability to handle finances of others.

Jupiter in Ninth House: Optimistic, broad-minded, and logical. Good time for study and travel. Excellent time for lecturing.

Jupiter in Tenth House: Can be influential, especially in business and politics. Success in your career, with good financial returns. Could do well on the stage.

Jupiter in Eleventh House: Enjoyment comes from a large number of friends and acquaintances. Popular, with a great social life. Plans are falling into place.

Jupiter in Twelfth House: Psychic powers come to the fore. Can help others without pushing yourself into the spotlight. Now is the time to be philanthropic.

Saturn in First House: Self-confident. Persistent. If afflicted, possible ill health. Beware of inhibitions cramping your style. If well aspected, will be very constructive and show yourself as solid and reliable.

Saturn in Second House: Will have to work hard to earn your money—nothing is free! However, you will learn and develop from this. Learn to budget.

Saturn in Third House: May have to take on some responsibility for siblings. There could be difficulties associated with education. The ability to work at problems and find solutions.

Saturn in Fourth House: Anxiety about aging and approaching old age. You feel restricted in your home life. Learn to discipline yourself.

Saturn in Fifth House: Difficulties with children and with your father, or another paternal figure. Little sense of humor. If afflicted, sexual inhibitions.

Saturn in Sixth House: May not entirely enjoy your work, but you will be good at it. If afflicted, could suffer from depression and even ill health. Try not to be despondent.

Saturn in Seventh House: A delay in marriage or partnership plans. Ambitious but need to learn to be more affectionate. Loyal and conscientious.

Saturn in Eighth House: Psychic powers come to the fore. If afflicted, can become moody and self-opinionated. If well aspected, responsible and can handle problems with seemingly little effort.

Saturn in Ninth House: Scientific and studious. Frustration due to lack of education. Good at studying but, if afflicted, tend to mental exhaustion. A loss connected with long distance travel.

Saturn in Tenth House: Able to hold a responsible position but, if afflicted, can carry a grudge, which will not help you. You demand recognition but feel loneliness.

Saturn in Eleventh House: Do not enjoy a lot of friends but the ones you have are good, loyal friends; many of them are much older. Frequent mental wrestling with problems.

Saturn in Twelfth House: A period of quiet—almost of disenchantment. Will feel morbid (especially if under affliction) and seek seclusion. Will feel the weight of the world on your shoulders, but it is mainly in your own mind.

Uranus in First House: Independent and inventive, with scientific leanings. Freedom-loving but somewhat erratic. If afflicted, may be stubborn and have trouble getting along with others. Dislike restrictions. Eccentric.

Uranus in Second House: Good financial news. If well aspected, these advances could be long-lasting. Discover unusual ways to make money.

Uranus in Third House: Get a lot of sudden, inventive ideas. Love of travel. If afflicted, can be too outspoken and ideas can be too scattered to be effective.

Uranus in Fourth House: Possibility of relocation. Domestic upheavals. Need for emotional security. Under affliction, can be very disruptive.

Uranus in Fifth House: Love of gambling and speculation. Able to inspire others. Constantly changing love life, with unconventional views on sex.

Uranus in Sixth House: High-strung. Prone to circulatory problems, which may develop suddenly. An unpredictable worker. If afflicted, will have problems with coworkers.

Uranus in Seventh House: Believer in free love and open marriages. Like a partner who is eccentric in some way. Beware of marrying, or entering a partnership, too quickly. Under affliction, have a tendency to cruelty.

Uranus in Eighth House: Interest in the afterlife, and have unconventional views concerning it. Psychic abilities. If well aspected, may receive some money from an unusual and unexpected source. If afflicted, may suffer financial losses.

Uranus in Ninth House: Be careful: you are very accident-prone at this time. Beware of a potential nervous breakdown. Urge to travel but, if afflicted, could encounter accident while traveling. If well aspected, could encounter very unusual and exciting events while traveling.

Uranus in Tenth House: Difficulty taking orders from others and have thoughts of self-employment. Farsighted and could be a good leader. Interested in unusual careers. Independent and original.

Uranus in Eleventh House: Enjoy societies and organizations; have unusual ideas for reform of such groups. Friends come and go without you really noticing.

Uranus in Twelfth House: Beware of deceit and treachery around you. Attracted to the unusual. If afflicted, interests could lead to being misunderstood and could jeopardize your reputation.

Neptune in First House: There is a need to be firm and decisive. It is very easy to drift and dream. Establish definite objectives and plan for the future. Try to think positively.

Neptune in Second House: A tendency to spend money on needless, frivolous items. Finances are uncertain at this time, so try to budget carefully.

Neptune in Third House: Great interest in the occult. Imaginative and intuitive. Fail to express yourself well or display your emotions. Try to develop concentration.

Neptune in Fourth House: Be on the lookout for theft—increase security. Enjoy artistic surroundings. If afflicted, misunderstandings can arise in family matters.

Neptune in Fifth House: Faults in loved ones are not seen. Overindulgence of sensual pleasures. Inspiration from movies and television. Susceptible to seduction.

Neptune in Sixth House: Disorganized. Love being alone. Need to serve others, in some way. If afflicted, beware of food poisoning and unusual health patterns.

Neptune in Seventh House: A need for companionship, but choice of partners is unusual. Difficulty judging others' character. If afflicted, there may be unexpected problems. There may be disappointment in marriage.

Neptune in Eighth House: Powerful intuition. Good imagination. Finances, especially those involving a partner, may show unexpected fluctuations.

Neptune in Ninth House: Strongly imaginative. Very interested in travel. You form your own philosophies. Intuitive.

Neptune in Tenth House: Artistic. Unusual careers attract. Capable of becoming famous. Good leadership. Many possible career changes.

Neptune in Eleventh House: Beware of deception and fraud. Can easily be led astray. Open to seduction. Idealistic.

Neptune in Twelfth House: Creativity prevalent. Artistic abilities, especially in the field of poetry. Intuitive and psychic. If afflicted, subject to self-deception and living in a fantasy world.

Pluto in First House: Skeptical—needing proof. Idealistic, imaginative, and sensitive. If afflicted, beware of major and minor crises, changes, and upheavals.

Pluto in Second House: Finances are unstable. Don't be too free with your money. Attracted to items for their aesthetic appeal. Income may come from more than one source.

Pluto in Third House: Petty jealousies in the family. Don't be too sensitive. Strong intuition. You have a searching, penetrating mind.

Pluto in Fourth House: Great interest in family history. Tendency to be untidy in the home. If afflicted, will experience sudden upheavals in family life. Learn to cooperate with other family members; don't be dictatorial.

Pluto in Fifth House: Enjoyment from video movies and the cinema. A love of adventure. Beware of gambling tendencies. If afflicted, may become jealous and dominating in romantic affairs.

Pluto in Sixth House: Interest in the medical field. Be careful not to abuse prescribed drugs. Watch what you eat—it could bring about food poisoning. Don't expect too much from others.

Pluto in Seventh House: Learn to work well with others. Possibility of a big change in your life, due to the influence of another. May become involved with a religious or artistic partner.

Pluto in Eighth House: A number of small crises, including economic upheavals. Look for professional help with your finances. Powerful imagination and intuition.

Pluto in Ninth House: Travel-minded; seeking adventure. Involved in the occult. If afflicted, guard against religious fanaticism.

Pluto in Tenth House: A variety of opportunities with your career, including changes of fields. Independence is exerted. Beware of becoming dictatorial. Guard against possible scandal.

Pluto in Eleventh House: An urge to change the world. Could get caught up in cults and mass hysteria. Carefully examine any claims made by others. A lot of good friends but, if afflicted, could be led astray by them.

Pluto in Twelfth House: Extremely sensitive. Try to understand yourself before judging others. If afflicted, subject to nervous tension and petty jealousies.

Note: If a coin lands on the line between two houses, it is "on the cusp," and both house meanings need to be read.

Part Three

COINS FOR TAROT
AND DOMINOES

INTERESTINGLY, COINS CAN BE USED in much the same way as tarot cards and dominoes; they can be used to determine the answer to a question or to get a general reading for what the future may hold. It is the equivalent of drawing and reading tarot cards to get an idea of the forces at work around you.

Tarot Effect

Take fourteen of each of four different coins: fourteen A, fourteen B, fourteen C, and fourteen D. Place all fifty-six coins in a large jar (a fish bowl is good for this), a box, or another container. Shake them up, and make sure to mix them well.

After contemplating on your question(s), reach into the jar and grasp a handful of coins. Bring them out and lay them on the table. Separate them into their four denominations. You might (for example) have eight A, three B, ten C, and two D. Within these groups, you might have three heads and five tails of A, two heads and one tail of B, four heads and six tails of C, and two tails of D.

To interpret, you can equate each of the denominations with each of the suits of a deck of tarot cards. For instance, A is Cups, B is Staves (or wands, in many decks), C is Pentacles, and D is Swords. (Decide for yourself, beforehand, which is which. I'd suggest always staying with the same correspondences.) The heads are upright cards and the tails are reversed cards. From this, then, your handful of coins has presented you with the equivalent of the 3 of Cups upright, the 5 of Cups reversed, the 2 of Staves upright, the Ace of Staves reversed, the 4 of Pentacles upright, the 6 of Pentacles reversed, and the 2 of Swords upright.

Let's look at tarot meanings, in order to read these coins.

74

Cups

Ace: Fertility; productivity. Beginnings. Love and joy.

Reversed: False hopes; instability; hesitancy.

Two: Balance. Partnership in business or love. Reciprocity. Friendship.

Reversed: Misunderstanding. Unstable partnership.

Three: Success; plenty; luck and good fortune. A time for celebration. Good hospitality.

Reversed: Overindulgence. Crumbling of dreams just when they seemed attainable.

Four: Dissatisfaction. Frustration. Scorn. Disappointment. Time for reevaluation.

Reversed: Renewed ambition and new ideas. Doors opening.

Five: Pessimism. Absorption in losses, forgetting gains. Breakup of relationship. Loss of friendship. Absorption in sorrow.

Reversed: Reawakening. The return of a lost friend or lover. Optimism.

Six: Memories of the past, particularly of childhood. Renewed acquaintance with childhood friend. Plans for the future. New ideas; renewed enthusiasm. Gifts, given and received. Pleasure; happiness.

Reversed: Unhealthy obsession with the past. Need to update; to bring life in line with reality. Possible inheritance from long-forgotten source.

Seven: Mystery. Dreams becoming a reality. An unexpected turn of events. Illusion; false perception. Beware of deception.

Reversed: Unlimited choices. Need to follow-up on unexpected success.

Eight: Fresh start. Turning away from past success to go in a new direction. Adventure and opportunity. Abandoning material success. Seeking spirituality. Disappointment in love, leading to new ventures and sudden-found courage.

Reversed: New interests. Turning from the spiritual to the material. Plans frustrated.

Nine: Material success and satisfaction. A time to sit and enjoy the fruits of labor. Recognition and honor. Unlimited opportunities.

Reversed: Falling short of goals. Promises unfulfilled. Envy of others. Jealousy. Dreams shattered.

Ten: Absolute bliss and contentment. Close friends and family. Dreams fulfilled. Success in all things. Sharing and companionship. Fertility and expansion.

Reversed: Loss of love and friends. Betrayal. A goal almost reached but not attainable. Restriction. Imprisonment.

Page (11): News of new arrival(s). Possibility of new venture. Orders to be carried out. Service to another.

Reversed: Bad news. Superficiality. Straying from the intended path. Unexpected obstacles.

Knight (12): A proposal, proposition, or invitation. Chance to join forces or amalgamate. Opportunity. Possibility of expansion. A message coming.

Reversed: Fraud; trickery. Beware of temptation. Care should be taken, especially with any form of contract. Sensuality. Diversion.

Queen (13): Foresight. A woman with a vision. Loyalty and dedication. Security. Pleasure. A person (probably a woman) with excellent judgment in authority. Good, long-range planning. Ability to handle business; real estate.

Reversed: Instability. Someone not to be relied upon. Dishonesty or incompetence. The failure of long-term plans.

King (14): A skilled lawyer or administrator. Consideration; responsibility. Creativity. Long-term plans involving travel. Generosity; compassion.

Reversed: A dictatorial administrator. Craftiness to the point of dishonesty. Duplicity. Calm before the storm.

Staves

Ace: Overabundance. Fertility trying to burst forth. Ideas, inventions, and projects—the time to start any fresh projects. Confidence and ability to start anything new; go in a different direction.

Reversed: False starts and confused plans. Cancellation of planned enterprises. Infertility and sterility.

Two: A good time to make plans. Solid foundation, especially to relationships. Desire to travel. Satisfaction. Wealth, position, and prestige.

Reversed: Frustration and restlessness. Unsure of plans. Changing circumstances. Inconsistency. Uncertainty.

Three: Partners and friends. Support. Encouragement. Dare to dream. Hope. Confidence.

Reversed: Caution, especially when help is offered. Watch for ambiguity. Do not rely on others.

Four: Vacation earned. Possible romance or marriage. Partnership offered. Peace and prosperity. Opportunity to celebrate.

Reversed: Need for a vacation. Frustration in romance. Incompletion. Loneliness.

Five: Competition. You will have to struggle or fight for what you want. Obstacles. Lawsuits. You can get lost in a crowd. You need to better assert yourself to be recognized.

Reversed: Opportunities. Victory within sight. Recognition. End of a time of struggling.

Six: Hard-won victory. Recognition and honors. Advancement. Leadership. Appreciation. Election to office. Promotion.

Reversed: Unexpected delay for expected rewards or payment. Unexpected defeat. Loss of position. Abuse of power.

Seven: Opposition. Need to meet opponents face-to-face. Minor victories leading to eventual success. Constant irritations. Fierce competition. Be alert and watch out for those working against you.

Reversed: Threats against you. Indecision. Weakness. Possibility of being thrown off balance.

Eight: Messages from afar. Rapid advancement. Journey, possibly by air. Approach or arrival. Needed vacation. Time for rest and recuperation. Expected news.

Reversed: Silence . . . expected messages not received. Stirrings of jealousy. Stagnation. Canceled journey.

Nine: Respite. Needed rest between struggles. Minor victory, with other battles ahead. Obstinacy. Refusal to admit defeat. Change of plans. Recuperation needed.

Reversed: Bitter defeat. Loss of reserves. Breakdown of health. Trickery. Outmaneuvered.

Ten: Surprising strength; unexpected reserve. Struggling on to the end. Hard-fought victory. Over-burdened. Poor judgment. Goal in sight but not necessarily attainable. Realization of loss of youth.

Reversed: Sapping of strength. Loss of support. Exhaustion. Surprisingly overburdened.

Page (11): A messenger with good news. Love of beauty. Aspirations to grandeur. Quick temper, but also quick to love. Pride.

Reversed: Cruelty. Instability. Bad news. Vanity, egotism, and narcissism. Distraction.

Knight (12): Youthful enthusiasm. Energy. Ready for anything. A good friend or a lover. Beware of being too enthusiastic; try not to get carried away. Pent-up emotions. Impatience with restraint.

Reversed: Jealousy. Loss of energy. Rudderless—unable to settle on a direction. Disinterest.

Queen (13): Kindness and generosity. Motherliness. Caring authority. Sound business and financial management. Love of animals. Domesticity. Respect. Success.

Reversed: Domination. Vengeance. Unreliable. False pretensions.

King (14): Noble and loyal. Family man. Honest. Knowledgeable. Influential. Staid marriage with at least one child. Closeness to nature.

Reversed: Ruthless. Severe. Ill-tempered and intolerant. Abuse of authority.

Pentacles

Ace: Bliss. The start of prosperity. Beauty. Pleasure. Friendship. The world awaits you!

Reversed: False starts. Promise turns to disappointment. Failure. Loss of beauty. Greed.

Two: Dexterity. Ability to juggle people and situations. Need to make a choice. Wisdom in choosing. Spontaneity. Gaiety. Sense of humor. Desire to travel. Spirituality.

Reversed: Forced laughter. Clumsiness. Difficult decisions to be made. News from abroad.

Three: Supervisory skills. Artistic ability. Manual skills. Craftsmanship. Pride in work. Willingness to take direction.

Reversed: Lack of skill. Laziness. Inability to direct. Ignorance.

Four: Thriftiness. Inheritance. Beware of becoming miserly. Material success. Loneliness and lack of friends. Position of authority bought. Hollow victory.

Reversed: Spendthrift. Inability to hold on to money. Loss of material wealth. Financial setbacks.

Five: Homelessness, though only temporarily. Destitution. Loss of material wealth, friends, and home. Unexpected promise of good things to come. Abandonment.

Reversed: Slow reversal of bad fortune. Receive charity. Regain losses. Promise of future employment.

Six: Wealth. Generosity. Charity. Willingness to help others who are less fortunate. Good investments. Good at making balanced decisions.

Reversed: Ostentatious. Flaunting wealth. Possibility of loss of wealth. Bribery. Indebtedness.

Seven: Rest after labors. Investment for long-term returns. Anxiety. Apprehension. Needed vacation. Speculation. Tendency to daydream.

Reversed: Small return for large amounts of labor. Frustration. Cancellation of plans.

Eight: Steady (sometimes tedious) work. Labor of love. Diligence. Skill at trade. Pride in work. Apprenticeship. Steady employment. Menial tasks.

Reversed: Failure to live up to your ambitions. Vanity. Duplicity. Counterfeiting.

Nine: Earned leisure and wealth. Position and authority. Time for leisurely pursuits. Money to indulge in hobbies. Love of formal gardens and landscaping. Master or Mistress of the house.

Reversed: Caution needed. Possibility of robbery. Sudden loss of wealth and position. Lack of time for personal pursuits.

Ten: Wealth and position. Possible inheritance. Large family and many friends. Respected head of household or business. Expanding investments. Rewards after long years of service.

Reversed: Family misfortune. Loss of income. Bad investments. Untrustworthy friends.

Page (11): Introversion. Tendency to daydream. Bearer of good news. Inventions and ideas. Love of the outdoors and outdoor activity. Ability to study and learn. Love of books.

Reversed: Bad news regarding loss of finances. Wasting time. Absentmindedness. Easily distracted.

Knight (12): Patience. Trustworthiness. Solidity. Good, close friendship. Support available if needed. Nobility. Acceptance of responsibility.

Reversed: Lack of responsibility. Inability to focus. Timidity and fearfulness. Loss of control.

Queen (13): The Earth Mother. Trust, love, and security. Power gently used. An iron hand gloved in velvet. Generosity and charity. Introspection.

Reversed: Neglect. Distrust. Fear of making decisions. Abuse of power. Suspicion.

King (14): Financier. Seasoned businessman. Mathematician. Man of honor and reliability. Recipient of many honors. Steady temperament.

Reversed: Gambler. Vanity. Bribery. Recklessness. Thriftless. Could be deeply involved in illegal operations.

Swords

Ace: Fertility. Potential for all things. Triumph over adversity. Strength in love. Leadership.

Reversed: Sterility and infertility. Loss of leadership. Worthless victory.

Two: Decision time. Ability to judge carefully and fairly, weighing all things. Balance. Deadlock. Ignorance of possible problems. Aloofness. Introspection.

Reversed: Rapid movement, without considering the direction. Misjudgment. Betrayal.

Three: Love problems. Jealousy. Rivalry. Challenges to the affairs of the heart. Tears and disappointment.

Reversed: Confusion. Loss. Reunion of lovers. Barrenness.

Four: Banishment. Solitude. Sabbatical. Long, deserved rest after much activity. Quiet before festivities.

Reversed: Disturbed rest. Uneasy silence. Enforced inactivity.

Five: Small victory—one battle in the war. Defeat of enemies. Success through effort. Promotion.

Reversed: Misplaced pride. Possible defeat or loss. Shallow victory. Weakness.

Six: Escape from conflict. Relocation. Fall back to recuperate and reorganize. Seek reinforcements. A new beginning is possible.

Reversed: Stagnation. Dead end—no way out. Problems will get worse.

Seven: Partial, not total, success. Cunning. Stealth. Spying. Infiltration. Action without proper planning. Unstable situation. Distrust.

Reversed: Solid foundations. Trust. Reentrenchment.

Eight: Total inability to move. Surrounded by hazards. Restriction. Held prisoner. Initiation. Challenge. Bondage.

Reversed: Release. Freedom. Unbinding. Knowledge.

Nine: Apparent total defeat. Imprisonment. Retirement. Fear. Suffering, burden, and loss. Misery.

Reversed: Renewal. Healing. Rebirth. Vacation.

Ten: Betrayal. Ruin and utter defeat. End of plans. Total rejection. Collapse. Loss of all that was held dear.

Reversed: Learning by experience. Recovery after threat of collapse. Overthrow of opposing forces.

Page (11): Espionage. Diplomat. Government worker. Reversal of roles. Pretense. Dance, music, and the arts.

Reversed: Impostor. Distraction. Hidden strength. Traitor.

Knight (12): Impetuous advance. Strength without thought. Innocent courage. Misfortune. Unexpected ally. Hidden strength.

Reversed: Bullying. Inappropriate behavior. Wild destruction. Tyranny.

Queen (13): Mourning. Kindness but firmness. Intelligence. Wisdom. Ability to rule and judge. Infertility.

Reversed: Gossip. Unstructured government. Lax discipline. Deceit. Unreliability.

King (14): Strength, authority, and wisdom. Position and influence. Wise counsel. Law and order. Military strength and discipline. Thoughts, ideas, inventions, and plans.

Reversed: Distrust. Suspicion. Poor planning. Bad administration. Abuse of power. Maliciousness.

Let's return now to our example of drawn coins; we have the 3 of Cups upright, the 5 of Cups reversed, the 2 of Staves upright, the Ace of Staves reversed, the 4 of Pentacles upright, the 6 of Pentacles reversed, and the 2 of Swords upright. From this we might read them as follows:

There is a time for celebration coming, with great success and good fortune. At this celebration you may encounter a friend, or even a lover, from the past; someone with whom you had lost contact. There is reason for great optimism. This will be a good time to make plans for the future. You have a solid foundation on which to build, especially regarding relationships. You may have a desire to travel.

However, be prepared for false starts and possibly a cancellation of some kind. You should be thrifty but beware of becoming miserly. Some material success is possible. Later, there may be a period of loneliness.

There is the possibility of some loss of wealth, perhaps from indebtedness? Do you owe money? Beware of being ostentatious; do not flaunt any wealth you may have.

Decision time is approaching. You have the ability to judge carefully and fairly, weighing all things, but be aware of possible problems ahead. Introspection is always wise.

A reading based simply on the drawing and throwing of coins!

Domino Effect

This is using coins much like throwing dominoes. In a pouch, or a jar, place twelve coins; six of denomination A and six of B. Shake them up, then reach in and pull out a few. Let's say, for example, that you pull out five coins—three of A and two of B. This would be the equivalent of 3:2 in dominoes. If you pull out, say, six coins, all of them type A, then this is 6:0. Make a note of them, return them to the pouch, then mix and pick again. Do this three times in all. Let's say, for example, that your three draws give you 2:2, 6:1, and 4:0. The first is the past, the second the present, and the third the future. Below are the traditional meanings for the dominoes.

0:0 Loss and unhappiness. A dull life.

0:1 Encounter with a stranger who will cause some unhappiness.

0:2 The start of a new partnership that will, however, prove fruitless.

0:3 Wrong decisions and jealousy bring about problems.

0:4 Letter received, bearing bad news.

0:5 You will attend a funeral, though it is not the funeral of a relative.

0:6 Someone whom you thought to be a friend is responsible for spreading scandal about you.

1:1 Things are in perfect balance. Now is the time to make decisions.

1:2 You will lose money or property in the near future.

1:3 An unexpected discovery leads to a pleasant surprise.

1:4 If you wish to stay out of trouble, then now is the time to pay your debts.

1:5 The chance for a romantic, passionate, love affair.

1:6 Time to make a decision. . . . Time will tell whether or not it is a wise one!

2:2 Both your home life and your business life are on solid ground. Beware of upsetting either one.

2:3 Avoid taking any chances. Don't gamble—you'd be the loser!

2:4 All of your investments—financial and emotional—will double.

2:5 Increase. Profits in business or investment. Possibility of increased family.

2:6 You will receive a gift that will turn out to be extremely useful to you.

3:3 You will be aggravated upon learning of the marriage of an ex-love.

3:4 You will unexpectedly meet an ex-love you had almost forgotten.

3:5 A promotion is imminent.

3:6 You will be invited to a party and, if you go, will thoroughly enjoy it.

4:4 Unexpected money, coming in an unexpected way.

4:5 A gamble pays off—but don't push your luck!

4:6 Be careful; you will be involved in a lawsuit.

5:5 To your great advantage, you will relocate.

5:6 You are in a position to help others and should do so.

6:6 Success in all things.

With the three drawings made, 2:2, 6:1, and 4:0, we can read the past, present, and future as follows:

In the past, both your home life and your business life have been on solid ground. Now is the time to make a decision. Consider carefully, for only time will tell whether or not it is a wise one. Prepare yourself for a letter, coming in the future, which will contain some bad news.

Another method is to concentrate on a question and then make seven drawings of the coins; equivalent to seven dominoes. This will give a reading of considerable depth.

Any number or combination of numbers of drawings can be used to answer questions and to gain insight.

Part Four

COINS FOR
THE I CHING

THE I CHING (PRONOUNCED "YEE JING"), as a form of divination, was traditionally devised by a legendary Chinese sage named Fu Shi, over 4,500 years ago. The *Shu Ching*, China's oldest history book, states that the I Ching was consulted by ancient governments—its judgment being taken over that of the emperor!

Although many traditionalists throw yarrow stalks to arrive at the necessary hexagrams of interpretation, coins have also been used for many hundreds of years. The Chinese coins are circular, with a square hole in the center (this was so they could be carried threaded onto a stick). The round, outer shape of the coin stands for *Ch'ien*, heaven, while the square hole represents *K'un*, earth. One side has four characters;

this is the *yang*, or positive, side. The negative side, the *yin*, originally had no characters; however, two characters were added—the Man Chou characters—in the Man Ch'ing Dynasty.

The ancient Chinese philosophers did not believe in a motionless universe; they felt it was constantly changing (hence the name "The Book of Changes" for this oracular method). Changes happen constantly in life, depending upon the operation of fate. However, if you can see the future, the workings of fate might be influenced. The I Ching allows you to do just that.

As with the seasons of the year, the changes are cyclical: joy – sorrow – joy – sorrow; wealth – poverty – wealth – poverty; success – failure – success – failure; and so on. The I Ching can tell you where you are in the cycle so you can see what lies ahead and plan accordingly.

In earliest times, it was felt that the Chinese oracle worked with great simplicity: an unbroken line was used to indicate *yes* and a broken line to indicate *no*.

Yet it soon became obvious that this could be inade-
quate for the majority of questions. The broken and
unbroken lines were therefore joined in combinations
of three, which gave eight possible arrangements, or
trigrams. A meaning was given to each of these:

Trigram	Name	Meanings
☰	Chi'en	Heaven. Male. Creative. Active.
☷	K'un	Earth. Female. Passive. Receptive.
☳	Chên	Thunder. Peril. Movement.
☵	K'an	Unstable Water. Pit. Danger.
☶	Kên	Mountain. Arresting Progress.

Trigram	Name	Meanings
≡≡	Sun	Wood. Wind. Gentle Penetration.
≡≡	Li	Fire. Beauty. Brightness.
≡≡	Tui	Lake. Marsh. Satisfaction.

If two of the trigrams are placed one above the other (Upper Trigram and Lower Trigram), you get a hexagram. It is then possible to create sixty-four combinations, and these are what are used for answering questions.

When consulting the I Ching, the hexagrams are built-up line by line. This is done by tossing the three coins, but first, you must decide on your question and concentrate, appropriately, on it for a few moments. Then do the first toss of the coins. Any three coins of equal size can be used: 3 quarters; 3 old English pennies; 3 of any coin with a distinctive head and tail.

Most people who are serious about doing the I Ching will purchase the traditional Chinese coins. Many occult supply stores sell them and they can easily be found at coin shops or numismatic stores.

The hexagram is built-up from its foundation; from the bottom. Heads score 3 and tails score 2. A throw might give you 3 tails = 2 + 2 + 2 = 6. Sixes and 9s are what are known as a *moving line*, and are shown as such: —X— or —0—. You might get 2 heads and 1 tail: 3 + 3 + 2 = 8. Eight is a broken line: ___ ___. Even totals are yin and odd totals are yang.

Here are the possibilities:

Coins	Score	Representation
3 tails	6	—X— (yin, moving line)
2 tails, 1 head	7	—— (yang)
1 tail, 2 heads	8	— — (yin)
3 heads	9	—0— (yang, moving line)

A moving line is interesting in that it is *in the process of change*, and the change is to its opposite. For example, if you get a 9 moving line, although it is a yang (all heads), it is in the process of changing into a yin: from 9 to 8. Similarly, a 6 moving line is in the process of changing from a yin into a yang: from 6 to 7. The result of all this is that although you might have thrown a hexagram that answers your question (as it will), that answer is actually unsettled; the hexagram is in the process of changing into a different hexagram! You then change those moving lines to their opposites, to the next progression up or down (6 to 7 or 9 to 8), and read the interpretation for *that* hexagram; this will give you an indication of what the changes are leading to in the future.

This may sound a little complicated at first, but it comes easily with a little practice, and is a wonderful insight into not only the present circumstances but also the probable change in the immediate future.

To begin, cup the coins in your hands and shake them up. It is better to shake them in your hands than it is to shake them in a container, since they will absorb your energies—and the energies of the question—as you handle them. Throw them down and note, on a piece of paper, the resulting combination. Remember that the first throw is the bottom line of the hexagram, and that you work your way up to the top line.

Each of the hexagrams has a number, which is then looked up in The Book of Changes. The answer to your question is found there. On the following page is a chart for finding the number of a particular hexagram. Look along the top for the Upper Trigram and down the left side for the Lower Trigram. Where they meet on the chart is the number of the hexagram. For example, K'un (on the top line) and Sun (left-hand column) give you hexagram 46.

Upper Trigram

Lower Trigram	Ch'ien	Chên	K'an	Kên	K'un	Sun	Li	Tui
Ch'ien	1	34	5	26	11	9	14	43
Chên	25	51	3	27	24	42	21	17
K'an	6	40	29	4	7	59	64	47
Kên	33	62	39	52	15	53	56	31
K'un	12	16	8	23	2	20	35	45
Sun	44	32	48	18	46	57	50	28
Li	13	55	63	22	36	37	30	49
Tui	10	54	60	41	19	61	38	58

Note: Pronunciation is as follows: Ch'ien = chee-an; Tui = dway; Li = lee; Chên = jen; Sun = soon; K'an = cun; Kên = gen; K'un = kwen; I Ching = yee jing

Attributes of the Trigrams

Ch'ien: Father. Creative. Strong; horse; heaven.

Chên: First son. Arousing. Movement; thunder; dragon.

K'an: Second son. Abysmal. Water; danger; pig; the pit.

Kên: Third son. Immobile. Mountain; hard; obstinate.

K'un: Mother. Receptive. Earth; cow/mare; yielding.

Sun: First daughter. Gentle. Wood; wind; cock; penetration.

Li: Second daughter. Clinging. Fire; eye; brightness; clarity.

Tui: Third daughter. Joyful. Lake; marsh; mouth; sheep; pleasure.

To give you a brief example, let's say that your throws were: 2 tails/1 head; 3 heads; 1 tail/2 heads; 1 tail/2 heads; 3 tails; 2 tails/1 head. This would give you the following:

The Upper Trigram is Kên and the Lower Trigram is Tui. Looking down the Kên column to the Tui line we find the number 41. 41, then, is the number of the hexagram for this throw of the coins; this is the number you look up to get the answer to the question you were asking when you threw the coins.

However, in your throws you have two moving lines: the second (next to bottom) line is a 9 total; a yang moving line ——0—— . In other words, although it is an unbroken line, it is in the process of becoming a broken line (yin): 8. Similarly, your fifth throw of

three tails is a 6 and another moving line: —X—.
This time it is a broken line (yin) in the process of
becoming an unbroken line (yang): 7. When the two
lines change, you will have a different hexagram,
which will look like this:

This gives you an Upper Trigram of Sun and a Lower
Trigram of Chên. Looking across the top of our table
to Sun and then down to Chên, we find the number
42. This hexagram must also be read to give the full
answer to your question, and is the resolution to the
first hexagram.

The Hexagrams

The Chinese Book of Changes has been translated into English by a number of scholars, most notably Richard Wilhelm and Cary F. Baynes, John Blofeld, Da Liu, and further interpreted by many other authors. Their books (see Bibliography) should be consulted for a more detailed investigation and study of the I Ching.

Hexagram 1

- *Ch'ien:* The creative principle
- Double creativity, activity, heaven
- Grandfather

——————— Ch'ien

——————— Ch'ien

This is the best indication of success, no matter what you are trying to achieve. Health, wealth, luck, and general good fortune are indicated. A complete set of unbroken lines shows that the "superior person" is capable of benefiting from any endeavor, as long as you are firm in that endeavor. You are powerful enough not to have to call upon anyone else's aid. It is, however, important that you remain on the straight and narrow path; that you are correct in all dealings and true in all your relationships.

Hexagram 2

- *K'un:* The passive principle
- Double earth, devotion, receptivity
- Grandmother

```
———  ———
———  ———    K'un
———  ———
———  ———    K'un
```

The full set of broken lines indicates harmony, but *passivity* is the keyword here. You may go astray at the start of projects but will get your bearings and return to the true path. It is necessary to submit to recognized authority, so initiative should be kept at a low ebb. You should be cautious in relations with youngest sons, yet strive to cultivate relations with oldest daughters. Open up your mind and embrace all things.

Hexagram 3

- *Chun:* Initial difficulty
- Thunder, movement; unstable water, a pit, danger
- Oldest son/second son.

```
___  ___
_____   K'an
___  ___
_____   Chên
```

Caution is the watch word. Progress and success will be gained by being firm. Nothing should be undertaken lightly. Be wary and you will be able to see the danger ahead and avoid it. Exercise patience. Don't hesitate to seek advice, from any and every quarter. This may be the time to reexamine your priorities and your plan of action. Try to come up with a better plan for the future.

Hexagram 4

- *Mêng:* Youthful inexperience or immaturity
- Unstable water, a pit, danger; mountains, delay
- Second son/youngest son

```
━━━━━━━━━
━━━  ━━━   Kên
━━━  ━━━
━━━━━━━━━
━━━  ━━━   K'an
```

Be resolute in your conduct. New projects need to be carefully nourished. Be wary of ignorance, stubbornness, youthful pride and arrogance, inexperience, and scorn of knowledge. To teach, do not seek out youth, but if youth approaches you, then give advice. However, only do so once; don't waste time and effort in repetition. With the right attitude, you will be assured of success.

Hexagram 5

- *Hsü:* Waiting
- Creativity, activity, heaven; unstable water, a pit, danger
- Father/second son

```
_____ _____
_____   K'an
_____ _____
_____
_____   Ch'ien
```

There will be great success if you are sincere in what you do, but you need to be patient and to wait, even though you may feel you need to act right away. Changes are in the process, and are all about you. Shifting forces will generate new ideas and fresh opportunities. Good fortune comes with firmness and persistence. Advancement brings achievement. Look at the present situation and procedure as a learning process.

Hexagram 6

- *Sung:* Conflict
- Unstable water, a pit, danger; creative, active, heaven
- Second son/father

```
━━━━━━━━━
━━━━━━━━━   Ch'ien
━━━  ━━━
━━━━━━━━━   K'an
━━━  ━━━
```

Caution. Your present path could lead you to conflict. It will not be advantageous to "cross the great stream"—be it a stream of thought, consciousness, tradition, or other. Good intentions alone are not enough. It could help to visit a "great man"; someone with power and influence. You need an inner adjustment; a new outlook on life. In your personal life, try to stay away from open confrontation at this time.

Hexagram 7

- *Shih:* The army (battle; competition; business rivalry)
- Unstable water, a pit, danger; earth, receptivity, devotion
- Second son/mother

```
═══ ═══   K'un
═══ ═══
═══ ═══
═══════   K'an
═══ ═══
```

There is some optimism. Weakness is in the lines, but also harmony. A seasoned leader is needed, someone who is firm and exact. Nourishment and feeding of the people is the best way to have an army of good soldiers in readiness; in other words, prepare well in advance for future contingencies. Be aware of others' needs and thoughts. Be firm in your resolve and know that what you are doing is right.

Hexagram 8

- *Pi:* Unity
- Earth, receptivity, devotion; unstable water, a pit, danger
- Mother/second son

```
━━━ ━━━
━━━━━━━   K'an
━━━ ━━━
━━━ ━━━
━━━ ━━━   K'un
━━━ ━━━
```

Reexamine your values and intentions. If you are on the true path, and your resolve is firm, then you will succeed; if you are hesitant, success will be slow in coming; if you are too slow in acting, failure will be the result. There is a chance that you have been chosen to be a special leader and take people forward on a positive course. If this is so, you must be absolutely certain of your own feelings and desires and must be sure that you are working for the common good.

Hexagram 9

- *Hsiao Ch'u:* Restraint from lesser powers
- Creative, active, heaven; wind, wood, gentleness
- Father/eldest son

```
━━━━━━━━━
━━━━━━━━━   Sun
━━━   ━━━
━━━━━━━━━
━━━━━━━━━   Ch'ien
━━━━━━━━━
```

It will seem as though your best efforts are thwarted and you are making no progress; there will eventually be progress leading to success, though not quite as you envisioned it. Although there are indications of further problems, they will not manifest. When you do attain success, it would be advantageous not to proclaim it loudly. Relations with eldest sons can be helpful.

Hexagram 10

- *Lü:* Treading carefully
- Lake, marsh, joy; creativity, activity; heaven;
- Youngest daughter/father

```
——————————
——————————  Ch'ien
———  ———
——————————  Tui
——————————
```

You may accidentally "tread on the tail of a tiger," but you will be lucky in that it will not bite. A hazardous position, but no failure as a result. You may, then, be cautiously optimistic. Success awaits you. This can be a very inspiring time for you, if you conduct yourself well. Beware of chaos and disorder.

Hexagram 11

- *T'ai:* Peace
- Creativity, activity, heaven; earth, receptivity, devotion
- Father/mother

```
━━━ ━━━
━━━ ━━━   K'un
━━━ ━━━

━━━━━━━
━━━━━━━   Ch'ien
━━━━━━━
```

The small and bad are gone; the good and the great have come. Good fortune and success. The hexagram is enigmatic. The active and bright principles of yang lie within while the dark, passive forces of yin are without—there is strength within and acceptance without. Expectation of slow but steady progress is indicated. There are ideal conditions in existence, at the moment, for new awakenings. Tread carefully and plan well. A good time for the start of new projects.

Hexagram 12

- *P'I:* Stagnation
- Earth, receptivity, devotion; creativity, activity, heaven
- Mother/father

```
————————
————————  Ch'ien
————————
—— ——
—— ——  K'un
—— ——
```

There is a negative omen, though it is more of an impasse than an outright failure. There is little expectation of good luck, but nothing is set in concrete. A great deal of patience and obedience is necessary at this time. There are strong counterforces present. The "superior person" must not slacken their righteous persistence.

Hexagram 13

- *T'ung Jên:* Fellowship with humankind
- Fire, brightness, beauty; creativity, activity, heaven
- Second daughter/father

```
─────────────
─────────────   Ch'ien
─────────────
───── ─────     Li
─────────────
```

A harmonious union is to come. If your goal is pursued with no taint of selfishness, then it will be achieved. The results will be long-lasting. It will be favorable to make a journey of some sort, though one involving the crossing of water will be especially efficacious. Do not slacken your righteous persistence.

Hexagram 14

- *Ta Yü:* Abundance
- Creativity, activity, heaven; fire, brightness, beauty
- Father/second daughter

```
————————
————  ————   Li
————————
————————
————————   Ch'ien
————————
```

Great progress and absolute success. The "superior person" suppresses what is evil and gives distinction to what is good. Prosperity and abundance are indicated, for families as well as for individuals. This is undreamed of. The only possible downfall could come from excessive pride, but this in extremely unlikely.

Hexagram 15

- *Ch'ien:* Humility
- Mountain, delays; earth, receptivity, devotion
- Youngest son/mother

```
———  ———
———  ———    K'un
———  ———
———  ———
———————     Kên
———  ———
```

Modesty and humility bring success, especially with new projects, which show great promise. Make modesty, and moderation, your special goals. Forces at work around you are in the process of balancing out, so extremes of any sort are not in evidence. Moderation should, therefore, be your key word. Watch your reactions to people and events and try not to overreact.

Hexagram 16

- *Yü:* Enthusiasm
- Earth, receptivity, devotion; thunder, movement
- Mother/oldest son

```
═══ ═══
═══ ═══   Chên
═══════
═══ ═══
═══════   K'un
═══ ═══
```

The hexagram means happiness and preparation, as well as enthusiasm. This is a condition of harmony, pleasure, and satisfaction. There is much optimism here. This is a time to install helpers and to start armies marching; however, beware of showing too much enthusiasm when starting new projects. This is a good sign for musicians and entertainers of all sorts.

Hexagram 17

- *Sui:* Following
- Thunder, movement; lake, marsh, joy
- Oldest son/youngest daughter

```
——— ———
———————  Tui
——— ———
——— ———
———————  Chên
```

The balance in the lines of this hexagram indicate long-range goals. If there are long verbal discussions, it is essential that decisions are made shortly after these discussions. Firm and consistently correct behavior is equally essential. There is no possibility of error. Plan ahead for the distant future, laying in stores in case of any future shortages.

Hexagram 18

- *Ku:* Stop decay
- Wind, wood, gentleness; mountain, delay
- Oldest daughter/youngest son

```
━━━━━  ━━━━━   Kên
━━━━━  ━━━━━
━━━━━  ━━━━━
━━━━━━━━━━━
━━━━━━━━━━━   Sun
━━━━━  ━━━━━
```

It is important to proceed with plans and, if necessary, to make a journey in connection with those
plans. Conditions may not be good now, but they will
improve. Some duties will be viewed as annoying,
even painful, but they must be completed and
brought to a satisfactory conclusion. Try to learn
lessons from any such problems.

Hexagram 19

- *Lin:* Approach
- Lake, marsh, joy; earth, receptivity, devotion
- Youngest daughter/mother

——— ———
——— ———   K'un
——— ———

——————————
——————————   Tui

Righteous persistence brings rewards. Cautious optimism may be allowed. Favorable results through the proper use of authority. Inspect, comfort, then rule. You are in a wonderful position to successfully carry out your plans, and to help others carry out theirs. Watch for misfortune in the eighth month.

•

Hexagram 20

- *Kuan:* Contemplation and observation
- Earth, receptivity, heaven; wind, wood, gentleness
- Mother/oldest daughter

```
━━━━━━━━━━
━━━━━━━━━━  Sun
━━━  ━━━
━━━  ━━━
━━━  ━━━  K'un
━━━  ━━━
```

The ablution has been made but the offering has not yet been given. Inspire trust and respect through sincerity and dignity. There is a division between those in authority and those under them. If you are the one in authority, put yourself in the other's place before acting. There is room for instruction. Remember that others are watching you as you watch those below you.

Hexagram 21

- *Shih Hô:* Biting through
- Thunder, movement; fire, brightness, beauty
- First son/second daughter

```
━━━━━━━
━━  ━━   Li
━━━━━━━
━━  ━━   Chên
━━━━━━━
```

A favorable time for legal proceedings. There are natural antagonisms between inferiors and superiors. There may be some small regret but there is no error. Stick to the letter of the law. Optimism is more prevalent than pessimism; there is good progress in the endeavor. This is a good time for reform. Seek out the barriers to your progress and help change them and remove them.

Hexagram 22

- *P'I:* Elegance; grace
- Fire, brightness, beauty; mountain, delay
- Father/first daughter

```
————————
——  ——   Kên
————————
————————
——  ——   Li
————————
```

Ornamentation is found in nature and is appropriate in society—but it should be secondary to that which is substantial. Don't be carried away by outward appearances. Don't spend so much time in beautifying that you do not prepare for coming problems. The sun shines on the mountains in beauty, but the darkness of night is not far behind! You may be flamboyant in your working, but there should be a hidden strength behind the outward display.

Hexagram 23

- *Po:* Disintegration
- Earth, receptivity, devotion; mountain, delay
- Mother/youngest son

```
━━━━━━━━━
━━━  ━━━    Kên
━━━  ━━━
━━━  ━━━    K'un
━━━  ━━━
```

Extreme caution is called for. You are at a stalemate; do not proceed in any direction at the moment. Force will not help. Delay any and all decisions. Carefully examine those who would undermine your position. Great patience is needed. Watch the opposition and competition carefully. Be kind and benevolent to others. This is a time for submissive action.

Hexagram 24

- *Fu:* Return
- Thunder, movement; earth, receptivity, devotion
- Eldest son/mother

```
━━  ━━
━━  ━━   K'un
━━  ━━
━━━━━━   Chên
```

Within seven days you will be back in an advantageous position; you will then be able to proceed in any direction you wish. There will be no opposition. Friends will come to you, to join you and lend their forces. Projects initiated on the heels of old failures will gain immediate success. You need to keep continually reassessing your position and your goals.

Hexagram 25

- *Wu Wang:* The unexpected
- Thunder, movement; creativity, activity, heaven
- Eldest son/father

```
━━━━━━━
━━━━━━━    Ch'ien
━━  ━━
━━  ━━    Chên
```

Simply do what you feel should be done, without detailed planning and goaling. The farmer plows in the spring even though he cannot predict what will happen in the fall. When he encounters difficulties, he must adapt to them. So let it be with you. Righteous persistence will bring its reward. Those opposed to righteousness will meet with injury.

Hexagram 26

- *Ta Ch'u:* The great taming force
- Creativity, activity, heaven; mountain, delay
- Father/youngest son

▬▬▬▬▬	
▬▬ ▬▬	Kên
▬▬▬▬▬	
▬▬▬▬▬	Ch'ien

There is much work to be done. There will be difficulties but you must struggle onward and not despair. Try to develop a friendship with problem people; they may be of help to you at a later date. This is a good time for travel. You are in possession of valuable information, whether or not you realize it; this is potential advancement for you. Now is the time to undertake new projects, carefully planning ahead for all contingencies.

Hexagram 27

- *I:* Nourishment
- Thunder, movement; mountain, delay
- Oldest son/youngest son

```
————— —————   Kên
————— —————

————— —————
—————————————   Chên
```

With firm correctness, there will be good fortune. An important advance will be made in one project. Beneficial gains require careful consideration of all aspects of the situation. You must look hard at what you plan to do and ensure that all efforts are directed to its completion. Trust your own judgment. Benefit from lessons learned in the past.

Hexagram 28

- *Ta Kuo:* Excess
- Wind, wood, gentleness; lake, marsh, joy
- Oldest daughter/youngest daughter

```
___ ___
_____
_____        Tui
_____
_____        Sun
___ ___
```

The present situation is becoming weighted with a
large number of considerations. A decision must be
made immediately, for it could quickly become an
explosive situation. Look for a way out; an avenue of
escape. Success is for those who remain resolute,
firm, and strong. You cannot ignore the situation.

Hexagram 29

- *K'an:* The abyss
- Doubly unstable water, a pit, danger
- Second son

```
____  ____
_____  K'an
____  ____
_____  K'an
____  ____
```

There is grave danger! Action is important, but think carefully before you act. An advance will be followed by achievement. The knowledge and experience you are about to gain will be invaluable in the future. Beware of trickery and deceit; watch out for theft. You could be injured or become involved in a serious dispute.

Hexagram 30

- *Li:* Fire; the clinging
- Doubly fire, brightness, beauty
- Second daughter

```
━━━━━━━━
━━━ ━━━    Li
━━━━━━━━
━━━ ━━━    Li
━━━━━━━━
```

The energy of the total far exceeds the energies of the separate parts. Make the best use of energy; don't fight it, but use it. External conditions are constantly changing. You must be ready to change with them. Be flexible—do not try to stick to predetermined plans. Cling to that which is available at the moment.

Hexagram 31

- *Hsien:* Influence
- Mountain, delay; lake, marsh,joy
- Youngest son/youngest daughter

```
———  ———
————————   Tui
————————
———  ———   Kên
———  ———
```

You must be open and receptive to whatever may present itself at the moment. A quiet openness allows you to be influenced, and also to influence. Both must be experienced to allow change. It will be to your advantage to seek advice from your superiors. The "superior person" keeps their mind free from pre-occupation and open to receive the advice of others.

Hexagram 32

- *Hêng:* Duration
- Wind, wood, gentleness; thunder, movement
- Oldest daughter/oldest son

```
_____  _____
_____       Chên
_____
_____       Sun
_____  _____
```

Remain firm and do not change your plans; however, do have a long-term goal in mind. Righteous persistence brings rewards. Continuity and unity are important. Avoid undisciplined actions. Listen to your inner voice. There will be successful progress and no errors.

Hexagram 33

- *Tun:* Withdrawal
- Mountain, delay; creativity, activity, heaven
- Youngest son/father

```
━━━━━━━━━
━━━━━━━━━   Ch'ien
━━━━━━━━━
━━━━━━━━━
━━━  ━━━    Kên
━━━  ━━━
```

Caution is needed. Do not try to contest an opponent directly but compromise, if necessary, and be prepared to retreat immediately, if you have to. Keep "small men" at a distance and in their place. Do not abandon your principles, but now may be a good time to take a sabbatical, review the past, and plan the future.

Hexagram 34

- *Ta Chuang:* The power of the great
- Creativity, activity, heaven; thunder, movement
- Father/oldest son

```
——— ———
——— ———   Chên
———————
———————   Ch'ien
———————
```

Advantage will come to the one who judiciously employs power and authority, yet strength should only be employed to do that which is right. This is a good time to advance. Exercise your power, but do not abuse it. You will find that you have unusual power, especially in personal relationships. Be responsible in all that you do; responsibility is a keynote.

Hexagram 35

- *Chin:* Progress
- Earth, receptivity, devotion; fire, brightness, beauty
- Mother/second daughter

```
—————————
————  ————   Li
—————————
—————————
————  ————   K'un
————  ————
```

Gratitude will be shown by a superior; gifts are a possibility. This is a very positive hexagram. There are good things—progress, rewards, advantages—in the immediate future. This is also a wonderful opportunity for good communication with family and in business; with family, unity is a blessing. This is a good time to examine your relationship with others: your equals, those above you, and those below you.

Hexagram 36

- *Ming I:* Darkening the light
- Fire, brightness, beauty; earth, receptivity, devotion
- Second daughter/mother

```
————  ————
————  ————   K'un
————————
————  ————
————————   Li
————————
```

You need to be patient and understanding. There will be benefits if you are able to stand up to your superior's inadequacies, but do not flaunt your knowledge. Be patient and await the right time. To act now would cause jealousy and difficulties. Time is an excellent teacher and now is a time to draw on past experiences. Expand your knowledge by study and research.

Hexagram 37

- *Chia Jên:* The family
- Fire, brightness, beauty; wind, wood, gentleness
- Second daughter/oldest daughter

```
————————————
————————————  Sun
————  ————
————————————
————  ————    Li
————————————
```

When everything is in its proper order, all is well. The family is headed by father and mother, then come the children, in the order of their seniority. If everyone knows their place, then things run smoothly and progress is made. It will be advantageous to assist those who have the greatest responsibility. One of the best ways to do this is to see that you attend to your own responsibilities.

Hexagram 38

- *K'uei:* Opposition/contradiction
- Lake, marsh, joy; fire, brightness, beauty
- Youngest daughter/second daughter

```
————————————
———— ————        Li
————————————
———— ————
————————————        Tui
————————————
```

There is a sense of contradiction and of opposition, yet there can still be progress in small matters. This is a time to examine both sides of every question. Others may see you as indecisive, or even contradictory, but take the time to examine. Strongly avoid discord. Watch out for distrust and suspicion among family members and business associates.

Hexagram 39

- *Chien:* Obstruction
- Mountain, delay; unstable water, a pit, danger
- Youngest son/second son

```
___  ___
_____    K'an
___  ___
___  ___
_____    Kên
___  ___
```

It will be advantageous to meet with a "great person." Don't be afraid to seek advice. Persistence is important. Obstacles in your path are part of the normal course of events and must be overcome in order for you to progress. If necessary, pause and build your strength before tackling the obstacle. Within yourself, these are inhibitions which, again, must be overcome.

Hexagram 40

- *Hsieh:* Liberation
- Unstable water, a pit, danger; thunder, movement
- Second son/oldest son

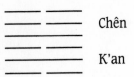

Chên

K'an

This hexagram follows from the previous one in that it shows relief of the tension and removal of the obstruction. Tension and anxiety are passing, both in business and in personal relationships. This is a time for a fresh new start. Put the past behind you and look to the future. In business, this is a good time for expansion. In your personal life, it is a good time to make a fresh start with loved ones.

Hexagram 41

- *Sun:* Decrease
- Lake, marsh, joy; mountain, delay
- Youngest daughter/youngest son

```
————————
——— ———    Kên
——— ———
————————    Tui
```

Take control of your emotions. Use whatever you have in hand to promote your interests. You could lose some income or property, though this may be through giving to others. Lack of profits from investments now means increased profits later. Remember that the pendulum swings and, though it may swing backward now, it will swing forward again later. Be totally involved and totally sincere in all you do.

Hexagram 42

- *I:* Increase
- Thunder, movement; wind, wood, gentleness
- Oldest son/oldest daughter

```
————————————
—————  —————   Sun
—————  —————
—————  —————   Chên
————————————
```

Much optimism. A good time to start new projects. An active time in business with prosperity ahead. There is a great deal of energy coming into your situation so make the most of it; work on new projects immediately, getting them off the ground. By showing your commitment constantly and consistently, you will meet with success.

Hexagram 43

- *Kuai:* Resolution
- Creativity, activity, heaven; lake, marsh, joy
- Father/youngest daughter

═══ ═══	
═══════	Tui
═══════	
═══════	
═══════	Ch'ien
═══════	

Beware of speaking too frankly and do not flaunt, or even show, your strength. Advance with caution. Defeat your enemies by making a firm, public resolution to advance as you wish to advance. Undermine them without doing battle with them. Change will only come with determination and steady, open progress.

Hexagram 44

- *Kou:* Encountering
- Wind, wood, gentleness; creativity, activity, heaven
- Youngest daughter/father

```
━━━━━━━━━
━━━━━━━━━   Ch'ien
━━━━━━━━━
━━━━━━━━━
━━━━━━━━━   Sun
━━━  ━━━
```

Not a good time to marry or join in partnership. If you are not careful, problems could escalate. Women hold the power at this time. There is negativity here, but negativity from which you can learn. New situations can arise suddenly and unexpectedly. You will encounter a person or situation that you cannot avoid. This is a time of temptation, so be on your guard.

Hexagram 45

- *Ts'ui:* Assembling
- Earth, receptivity, devotion; lake, marsh, joy
- Mother/youngest daughter

▬▬ ▬▬	Tui
▬▬▬▬	
▬▬ ▬▬	
▬▬ ▬▬	K'un

There is a celebration, party, or convention; a gathering together of many people. Whether you are the leader of this group or simply one of those involved, you should give all your energies to the good of the group and its advancement; you may be called upon to contribute or make a sacrifice. It will benefit you, in the future, if you do this. Prepare your forces for any unforeseen circumstances. A good time for marriage.

Hexagram 46

- *Shêng:* Ascending
- Wind, wood, gentleness; earth, receptivity, devotion
- Oldest daughter/mother

```
▅▅▅ ▅▅▅
▅▅▅ ▅▅▅   K'un
▅▅▅ ▅▅▅
▅▅▅▅▅▅▅
▅▅▅▅▅▅▅   Sun
▅▅▅ ▅▅▅
```

You will be recognized from an unexpected source, gaining public praise. Don't let this praise go to your head. This recognition could be in the form of a promotion, an increase in income, or merely an announcement of your worth. Business will prosper; blooming like flowers in the spring. As your business and personal life prosper, do not become prideful or arrogant; in addition, do not become lazy and careless.

Hexagram 47

- *K'un:* Adversity
- Unstable water, a pit, danger; lake, marsh, joy
- Second son/youngest daughter

```
____  ____
_____
____  ____       Tui
_____
                 K'an
____  ____
```

Cautious pessimism is here. Many outside forces are restricting progress and success. Don't allow the negative forces to destroy your character. Persistence in a righteous cause will eventually lead to success. You will feel exhausted and tired of battling the odds. There will be empty promises spoken; do not rely on the spoken word. Not a good time for marriage.

Hexagram 48

- *Ching:* The well
- Wind, wood, gentleness; unstable water, a pit, danger
- Oldest daughter/second son

```
―― ――
―――――   K'an
―― ――
―――――
―――――   Sun
―― ――
```

It may take the cooperation of several others to accomplish what you want. If you do not have success, you need to work at improving your career, your image, and your way of doing things. Togetherness is important. Knowledge is there for the taking; it is never-changing. All you have to do is reach out for it.

Hexagram 49

- *Kô:* Revolution
- Fire, brightness, beauty; lake, marsh, joy
- Second daughter/youngest daughter

▬▬ ▬▬	
▬▬▬▬▬	Tui
▬▬▬▬▬	
▬▬▬▬▬	
▬▬ ▬▬	Li
▬▬▬▬▬	

What may, on reflection, seem like an unwise alteration to your original plans, will actually turn out for the best. This change will come after careful reflection and recognition of circumstances. You will see what went wrong and how you should have planned for it in the first place. Learn by this experience. Do not be afraid of change, but be prepared for it.

Hexagram 50

- *Ting:* The caldron
- Wind, wood, gentleness; fire, brightness, beauty
- Oldest daughter/second daughter

```
————————
———  ———     Li
————————
————————
————————
———  ———     Sun
————————
```

This is a time when you can confidently express your opinion, but do not say anything vicious or contrary. You, and all those with whom you are associated, will attain success. Everything around you is developing positively at this time. Share knowledge, so that it may be meaningful—for knowledge kept to yourself is of little use.

Hexagram 51

- *Chên:* Thunder/shock
- Double thunder, movement
- Oldest son

| ▬▬ ▬▬ | Chên |
| ▬▬ ▬▬ | Chên |

There will be a favorable advance into a good position. It will startle others like a crash of thunder. It is time to shock a few people! This is a good time to examine your business and personal relationships. Unfinished business can cause trouble at this time; tie up all those loose ends as quickly as possible. You will find that you have a sudden burst of energy to get things done. Once the immediate shock is over, you will be able to look back and laugh.

Hexagram 52

- *Kên:* Stillness
- Double mountain, delay
- Youngest son

```
━━━━━━━
━━━ ━━━   Kên
━━━━━━━
━━━ ━━━   Kên
```

Rest when it is time to rest—as it is now—and act when it is time to act. In this way your progress will be even and constant. The truth is found in balance and harmony. This is a good time for meditation. Practice it; it will refresh body, mind, and spirit. Meditate on your goals and your plans for reaching them. This is a quiet time, not a time for action.

Hexagram 53

- *Chien:* Gradual progress; growth
- Mountain, delay; wind, wood, gentleness
- Youngest son/oldest daughter

```
━━━━━━━━━
━━  ━━━        Sun
━━━━━━━━━
━━  ━━━        Kên
━━  ━━━
```

Reward and advancement will soon be here. You should be aware of the true nature of daily life; it is neither positive nor negative. Be aware of all that is good in life. In order to reach your objective, you must take the slow, traditional path, which may seem too long to you. Be patient; there are no shortcuts.

Hexagram 54

- *Kuei Mei:* The marriageable maiden
- Lake, marsh, joy; thunder, movement
- Youngest daughter/oldest son

```
___  ___
___  ___   Chên
___  ___
_____
_____   Tui
```

This is not a good time for business. You are completely at the mercy of circumstance. Try to stay flexible. You are not in control of anything and must be ready to jump in any direction. Be frugal; this is not the time for spending. Marital disputes cannot be resolved at this time; it is well to remember that strife is as much a part of marriage as is bliss! Try to avoid any great arguments.

Hexagram 55

- *Fêng:* Abundance
- Fire, brightness, beauty; thunder, movement
- Second daughter/oldest son

——— ——— Chên
——————
——————
——— ——— Li

This is no time for sadness; you should be celebrating. There is development and progress. You may feel a sense of satisfaction at what you have achieved. Greatness, prosperity, and brilliance are suggested in this hexagram. However, you must make some judgments about where you are and where you wish to be. Get rid of any excess baggage.

Hexagram 56

- *Lü:* The wanderer
- Mountain, delay; fire, brightness, beauty
- Youngest son/second daughter

```
━━━━━━  ━━  ━━   Li
━━━━━━━━━━━
━━━━━━━━━━━
━━━━━━  ━━  ━━   Kên
```

Success in small things. A stranger, or exile, is shown in this hexagram. Sometimes he finds friends and shelter, but many times he must simply rough it and survive as best he can. If you are able to make the best of things, you will progress, step by step. Recognize when you have exhausted your resources and know when to move on. When it is time to move, it is time—so don't delay! All of this applies as much to "inner journeys"—to thoughts and imagination—as it does to physicality.

Hexagram 57

- *Sun:* Willing submission/gentle penetration
- Double wind, wood, gentleness
- Oldest daughter

```
━━━━━━━━
━━  ━━    Sun
━━━━━━━━
━━━━━━━━
━━━━━━━━    Sun
━━  ━━
```

You must allow the other person to influence you. Willingly submit in order to gain advancement in small things. Try to understand the thinking of your superiors. From this you will be able to recognize what is possible for you and what is not. At all times, keep your long-term goals in mind. Be prepared for a long, slow move forward to achieve your goals.

Hexagram 58

- *Tui:* Joyfulness
- Double lake, marsh, joy
- Youngest daughter

```
━━━  ━━━
━━━━━━━   Tui
━━━  ━━━
━━━━━━━   Tui
```

Caution brings success. Progress and attainment are shown. You will find encouragement. True joy depends upon strength within and firmness of purpose, manifested outwardly as gentle yielding. Keep the atmosphere around you one of gentleness and good will. Your success will be continuing.

Hexagram 59

- *Huan:* Dispersion
- Unstable water, a pit, danger; wind, wood, gentleness
- Second son/oldest daughter

```
————————
————————   Sun
————  ————
————————   K'an
————  ————
```

Progress and success. Travel, especially over water, is advantageous at this time. A good time to relocate. A good time to change careers. Business travel would be advantageous. Persistence will pay off, if the course is righteous. Marriage plans may be delayed, due to pressures of work for both parties. On all things, take time to look within; try to see the whole picture before making any decisions.

Hexagram 60

- *Chieh:* Limitation
- Lake, marsh, joy; unstable water, a pit, danger
- Youngest daughter/second son

```
━━━  ━━
━━━━━━━   K'an
━━━  ━━
━━━  ━━
━━━━━━━   Tui
━━━━━━━
```

There are limitations throughout nature, from the changing time of the year to the weather conditions. It is necessary to adapt to these changes in order to move ahead. Consider the limitations being presented to you, and how they are preventing your attainment of goals. Evaluate the situation so you can bypass any hindrances and move ahead. Where there are limitations that you cannot change, accept them rather than fight against them needlessly.

Hexagram 61

- *Chung Fu:* Insight
- Lake, marsh, joy; wind, wood, gentleness
- Youngest daughter/oldest daughter

```
————————————
——  ——            Sun
——  ——
————————————       Tui
```

Inward confidence and sincerity. Highly favorable circumstances. This is an excellent time to cross the waters, and to make use of an unloaded boat (or carrier of some kind). Don't be deceived into thinking that brute force and physical strength have any lasting impact. The advantage here is in selflessness; there is good fortune for those who appreciate its advantages.

Hexagram 62

- *Hsiao Kuo:* Conscientiousness
- Mountain, delay; thunder, movement
- Youngest son/oldest son

```
━━━ ━━━
━━━ ━━━   Chên
━━━━━━━
━━━━━━━
━━━ ━━━   Kên
━━━ ━━━
```

Progress and attainment. It is advantageous to be firm and correct. Action is called for in small projects, but hold off and show patience where larger projects are concerned. Listen to any ideas or suggestions from those beneath you; those whom you might normally consider inferiors. There might even be advantages in making small deviations from what would be considered normal. Maintenance is important at this time, as is restraint.

Hexagram 63

- *Chi Chi*: After completion
- Fire, brightness, beauty; unstable water, a pit, danger
- Second daughter/second son

```
____  ____
_____   K'an
____  ____
_____
____  ____   Li
_____
```

Progress and success in small matters. You've been very lucky to start with, but there may be some problems ahead. Plan for the future and guard against any negative eventuality. Persistence in a righteous course will pay dividends. A major project could be completed ahead of schedule, but in order to hold on to any gains, you will need to constantly be on top of things. This is also a good time to start new projects.

Hexagram 64

- *Wei Chi:* Before completion
- Unstable water, a pit, danger; fire, brightness, beauty
- Second son/second daughter

```
————— —————
————— —————   Li
————— —————

————— —————
—————  —————   K'an
————— —————
```

Progress and apparent success. The goal is within sight; within grasp. There is some humiliation, however, due to being overconfident. Beware of showing off. This is the moment just before what seems to be a certain victory. However, do not assume that, by achieving this goal, you will be home and free. Good judgment will still be called for and order must prevail. There are still many things that need to be done after the moment of victory.

Note: In the full translations of the I Ching (i.e., in Wilhelm's, Blofeld's, and Da Liu's books), more detailed interpretations of the hexagrams are given and these are followed by further interpretations of each individual line (starting at the bottom) of the hexagram. However, these line interpretations are not read for a second hexagram (following moving line adjustment). It is beyond the scope of this book to cover all the line interpretations as well as the main readings, so they have not been included.

Part Five

THE PRACTICE OF
COIN DIVINATION

YOU CAN, OF COURSE, take your coins and throw them, toss them, spin them, or whatever you like, though traditionally, it is good practice to treat divination as a ritual. Certainly, if you look upon divination as a magical practice—which it surely is—then it must be prepared for and performed in appropriate style.

Consecration of the Coins

The first thing necessary is to consecrate the coins. In magic, what is said and done is most powerful when it comes from the heart. It should be what is most appropriate for *you*, as an individual, which means not simply mouthing something that was written by someone else, perhaps hundreds of years ago in very different circumstances. I'll give an example; a basic ritual that might be performed. You may follow this exactly, or simply use it as a pattern to be adapted, rewritten by you to suit your own feelings and beliefs.

The small table on which you will place your coins, and other necessary items, we'll call an altar, but this ritual does not have to have religious overtones unless you wish them. Some may wish to direct their words and energies to a specific deity or deities, while others may wish to simply direct them to the universe, or turn them inward to their own personal power source. Whatever works for *you* is the best, correct way.

The altar can be any small table, chest, or even box, of convenient size, in front of which you may stand or kneel. If you wish, you may drape it with a cloth. On the altar, place a candle (color preference of your choice). Have a dish of incense on one side and a dish of water on the other, with the coins lying between the two. (The number of coins is, again, up to you. From what you have read in this book, you will have some idea of how many you are likely to need on a regular basis. You can always consecrate more later, if needed.) Many people like to put a pinch or two of salt in the water. I do this myself (see *Buckland's Complete Book of Witchcraft*, Llewellyn, 1986, and other of my books), since salt universally symbolizes the life force. Choose incense that appeals to you, but go with something that smells pleasant; not too pungent. Light the candle and the incense.

You may wish to draw a circle about the altar and to consecrate that (again, see *Buckland's Complete Book of Witchcraft* for details of this circle construction). Whether or not you do this, I suggest that, at the very least, you do the following:

Sit quietly for a moment. Breath deeply and evenly, allowing your mind to settle and your body to relax; lose any tension that may be present. Close your eyes and, as you breath deeply, concentrate on drawing positive energies to you on your in-breaths, and pushing away negative energies on your out-breaths. In your mind, see the positive energy as white light and *see* and feel it being drawn into your body. As you breathe out, see and feel the negativity, in the form of darkness (black, brown, or gray, for example) being forced out of your body. Keep this up until you feel that your whole body is filled with white light and all the negativity—all the little aches and pains, stress and strain—has been pushed away. We're not talking of demonic forces or black magic energies, since there is virtually no likelihood of them being present! We are simply talking of the many little distractions that might draw your attention away from the task at hand. In pushing these out, you will also be pulling in all positive energies that can only help, protect, and vitalize you.

When you feel your body is saturated with the white light, continue the breathing and drawing-in, but now see the light expanding beyond your body;

flowing out in a great white ball to fill the area in which you sit, kneel, or stand. See that ball of light enclose the altar and a good distance around it.

Now you may change your concentration to focus on the coins that lie before you. Take up the coins and hold them cupped between your two hands. Focus your energies on them and direct positive forces into them. You may say out loud (or simply concentrate in your mind) the following:

> These coins are the tools which I will use to divine the forces at work about me. Let them be filled with positive energies, that they will not lead me astray but will point me in the appropriate direction, to achieve that which I desire.

Dip your fingers in the water and sprinkle the coins, letting the drops of water fall on both sides of every one of them. Then hold them in the smoke of the incense. As you do this, say:

> Here I do cleanse these tools of any and all negativity, that they may be purified for the uses to which I may put them. Let the waters of life wash them clean and let the smoke of the incense connect them to the greater universe, that they may act as a conduit to the universal consciousness.

Hold the coins to your heart for a moment, feeling their energies blend with your own, then replace them on the altar. Sit for a few more moments in quiet contemplation, before extinguishing the candle and ending the ritual.

Many people keep the coins in a white silk or cotton cloth from then on. You may also keep them (and the cloth) in a bag, pouch (like the Gypsy *putsi*), or box of their own. I would further recommend that you carry the coins on you for a period of at least seven days. At night, sleep with them under your pillow. This will all help to imbue the coins with your own personal energies and make them very personal tools of divination for you.

This, as I have said, is a simple, basic ritual. Feel free to change it, if necessary, to suit your needs and feelings. Basically, all you are doing is cleansing the coins and dedicating them to a use as divination tools. Needless to say, after this they should not be used for any purpose other than divination.

Your Own Personal Coins

There is no reason why you shouldn't actually *make* coins to use for divination. In fact, any magical item that you make yourself will be far more powerful and potent than something store-bought, or made for another purpose and simply adapted. This is especially true of such magical items as athames (ritual knives), wands, swords, and the like, used in various forms of ritual magic. For coin divination, you may not feel that it is worth the effort of making them from scratch, since we are generally speaking in terms of simple divination. However, as I stated when talking of consecration, you can either treat the practice as simple divination, or you can look upon it as a special ritual, one that will put you more directly in touch with outside influences. If the latter, then make your own or, at the very least, personalize the coins you choose to use. We'll look at both possibilities.

Personalizing Existing Coins

You can personalize any coin, or medal, by engraving it; thus you put your energies into it. To engrave, you do not need any expensive equipment. In fact, you can even engrave—as many Gypsies do—with nothing more than a sharp nail! Actual engraving tools are not expensive; you can purchase electric engraving tools at a very low price. However, I would recommend, from the magical point of view, that you stick with a hand (nonelectric) engraver.

The engraving on the coin can be as simple as your initials or as complicated as a word or phrase written in one of the traditional magical alphabets. What is important is that you put your energies into the coin by doing some work on it. Some years ago I came upon a stash of old English farthings (a small coin, the value of one-fourth of a British penny), all engraved with a small pentagram, or five-pointed star, on the face. I imagine they had been prepared for something more than just divination tools, but the idea was the same. They had been imbued with someone's energies, or forces.

Making Coins

Coins are nothing more than circular pieces of metal with designs stamped or cast into them. Many metal-working shops have blanks that they throw out; pieces that have been stamped out of metal sheets destined for some other purpose. These can be quite suitable for divination coins. It's usually possible to obtain some of these blanks for virtually nothing—just speak to the shop manager. Similar pieces can sometimes be found at hardware stores. Many arts and crafts stores offer copper disks for enameling, which are perfect. I like to use various washers (the "spacers" placed between nuts and bolts), which can also be found at hardware stores. Washers are coin-size disks of metal, available in a variety of sizes, with a hole in the center. It's possible to find washers with large holes or with very small holes—the choice is yours. They come in various metals, from which you can choose. I favor brass; they are easier to engrave and, I feel, have a nicer feel to them than the steel washers. I do not care for aluminum washers at all; they are generally too light in weight for use as divination coins. I also suggest avoiding nickel coins, or coins with nickel centers.

Another attraction of the washers is that, because of the hole in the center, they are reminiscent of Chinese coins; albeit the Chinese coins have a square hole.

Taking your washer, you can then engrave whatever you like around both faces. You can, if you wish, copy the Chinese characters, or you can create your own personal symbols.

If you use a blank metal disk of one of the softer metals, you may be able to stamp initials or various designs into them, using metal design stamps or dies (found at arts and crafts stores) and a heavy hammer.

There is no reason why you should not make your "coins" out of ceramic, or even wood. These days a number of people make, and sell, runes of one sort or another made from these substances. The same principles can be applied to coins—burning designs into wood and engraving them into ceramics.

Another option is simply to paint the coins. Whether raw metal or actual coins, you can personalize them by using paints to place your initials or a design of your choice onto them.

That leaves you with a number of options from which to choose when you personalize the coins you will use for practicing coin divination. As I said earlier, you do not *have* to personalize them—any coins will do—but it makes them that much more special and adds your own personal energies to these divinatory tools.

You now have the tools you need and a wide variety of methods for using them. Coin divination is fun, easy, and accurate. Try it. Make it your divination choice and, above all, have fun!

Bibliography

Anderton, Bill. *Fortune Telling.* North Dighton, Massachusetts: JG Press, 1996.

Blofeld, John. *I Ching: the Book of Change.* New York: Dutton, 1968.

Buckland, Raymond. *Gypsy Fortune Telling Tarot Kit.* St. Paul, Minnesota: Llewellyn Publications, 1998.

_____. *Gypsy Witchcraft and Magic.* St. Paul, Minnesota: Llewellyn Publications, 1998.

Cheasley, Clifford W. *Numerology.* Boston, Massachusetts: Triangle, 1916.

Cheiro (Louis Hamon). *Cheiro's Book of Numbers.* New York: Arc, 1964.

Da Liu. *I Ching Coin Prediction.* New York: Harper & Row, 1975.

González-Wippler, Migene. *The Complete Book of Amulets and Talismans.* St. Paul, Minnesota: Llewellyn, 1991.

Gray, Magda, ed. *Fortune Telling.* London: Marshall Cavendish, 1974.

Jordan, Juno. *Numerology.* Marina Del Rey, California: DeVorss, 1965.

Lopez, Vincent. *Numerology.* New York: Citadel, 1961.

Sepharial (Walter Gorn Old). *The Kabala of Numbers.* Philadelphia, Pennsylvania: David McKay, 1945.

Wilhelm, Richard. Translated by Cary F. Baynes. *The I Ching.* Princeton, New Jersey: Princeton University Press, 1967.

Wing, R. L. *The I Ching Workbook.* New York: Doubleday, 1979.

REACH FOR THE MOON

Llewellyn publishes hundreds of books on your favorite subjects!
To get these exciting books, including those on the following pages, check your local bookstore or order them directly from Llewellyn.

ORDER BY PHONE
- Call toll-free within the U.S. and Canada, 1-800-THE MOON
- In Minnesota, call (651) 291-1970
- We accept VISA, MasterCard, and American Express

ORDER BY MAIL
- Send the full price of your order (MN residents add 7% sales tax) in U.S. funds, plus postage & handling to:

    Llewellyn Worldwide
    P.O. Box 64383, Dept. K089-2
    St. Paul, MN 55164–0383, U.S.A.

POSTAGE & HANDLING
(For the U.S., Canada, and Mexico)
- $4.00 for orders $15.00 and under
- No charge for orders over $100.00
- $5.00 for orders over $15.00

We ship UPS in the continental United States. We ship standard mail to P.O. boxes. Orders shipped to Alaska, Hawaii, The Virgin Islands, and Puerto Rico are sent first-class mail. Orders shipped to Canada and Mexico are sent surface mail.

International orders: Airmail—add freight equal to price of each book to the total price of order, plus $5.00 for each non-book item (audio tapes, etc.). Surface mail—Add $1.00 per item.

Allow 2 weeks for delivery on all orders.
Postage and handling rates subject to change.

DISCOUNTS
We offer a 20% discount to group leaders or agents. You must order a minimum of 5 copies of the same book to get our special quantity price.

(Visit our website at www.llewellyn.com for more information.)